For Ellery, Paige and Beckett.

You are the ultimate legacy.

Love,

Dad

Table of Contents

The Founder's Guide To Business Succession: Making It Last When You Leave

Library of Congress Catalog Number:

ISBN: 978-1533308665

First Edition

Printed in the United States of America

Prologue: A Really Useful Book On Succession Planning... Really.

If this were like most books on succession planning, I would have written a chapter on restricted stock plans, a chapter on the proper use of family limited partnerships, one on self cancelling installment notes, another chapter on employee stock ownership plans, one on gifting, one on buy sell agreements and maybe one more on ideal entity structures. Basically, I would have wasted your valuable time covering the technical pros and cons of the tools used in the succession-planning world. It would all be great information except for the fact that you'd have no idea what to do with it.

Instead, I set out to write a book on succession planning that you could actually use. This book consists of three parts. Part I will bring you the information about succession planning you really need to know. That means no jargon, no complex tax strategies and nothing you can't start using *right now*!

Part II spotlights the practical issues most likely to cause trouble in a succession plan so you can be on the lookout. These are what I refer to as "The Five Big Flubs". Each Flub earned its place on the list due to the sheer number of business owners who fall prey to it every year. Each time one of the flubs makes an appearance, that business owner is at risk of succession failure. They may not lose everything but it's unlikely they will end up accomplishing their goals.

Part III gives you perspective on succession planning from across the spectrum of other professionals. I've interviewed the trusted members of my client advisory board who shared their own stories, insights and advice from a collective 140 years of combined experience. These are industry experts who routinely charge thousands of dollars for the kind of insights you've just purchased for less than the cost of a tank of gasoline. Read on to discover where to begin when you're nearing the end.

Part I: Everything Founders *REALLY* Need To Know About Succession Planning.

Chapter 1: Where To Begin When You're Nearing The End

The Journal of the Korean Neurosurgery Society published a paper in 2014 titled *Emerging Surgical Strategies of Intractable Frontal Lobe Epilepsy with Cortical Dysplasia in Terms of Extent of Resection.*[1] Do you believe it would it be beneficial for me read that paper if I were a patient preparing to undergo brain surgery? It's vital information to be sure and I would certainly want my surgeon to have studied it along with as much other leading research as possible before cutting me open. However, it's probably not going to have a meaningful impact on my outcome as a patient to spend time reading the information.

There are simply too many variables requiring deep expertise on the technical side of the procedure for the information to be useful to me as a patient. In fact, it might even cause me to make some poor decisions when I'm struck by the full, detailed description of what that surgeon is actually going to be doing inside my head!

While developing a succession plan for your business isn't the same as performing neurosurgery, it's still a specialized field with its own jargon, specialized

[1] Jung-Hoon Shin, M.D.,1 Na-Young Jung, M.D.,1 Sang-Pyo Kim, M.D.,2 and Eun-Ik Son, M.D., Ph.D. Emerging Surgical Strategies of Intractable Frontal Lobe Epilepsy with Cortical Dysplasia in Terms of Extent of Resection. Journal of Korean Neurosurgery Society. 2014 Sep; 56(3): 248–253. Published online 2014 Sep 30. doi: 10.3340/jkns.2014.56.3.248

strategies and practitioners. There are plenty of books available on Amazon.com extolling the value of one strategy over another. I believe investing your time reading technically oriented books is more likely to decrease your odds of executing a successful transition than help you achieve your goal of exiting on your own terms. That makes this little book possibly the most useful guide to succession planning you will ever read.

The differences between organizations that last beyond their founder and those that don't are subtle. It often has little to do with revenues, tax management strategies, growth trends or marketing plans. Effective succession planning doesn't start with tactics or strategy. Effective succession planning starts with people. First and foremost, it is about the founder or "wealth creator". Just as the physical characteristics of parents are reflected in their children, the characteristics of the founder are reflected in his or her organization. It's not a 1:1 relationship, but the resemblance is striking.

We are currently in the portion of the business cycle in which investors and venture capitalists are leaving the public capital markets and pouring money into startups with tall valuations and short track records. Unbelievable amounts of personal and institutional wealth are being entrusted to organizations that likely have less staying power than a dandelion in a hailstorm. I believe economists will look back on many of these investments the same way they now look back on the dot.com era and wonder, "What were they thinking?!". Few of these companies will have the endurance to provide a long-term ROI to their investors and it won't be due to faulty marketing plans.

The companies that last (and the investors who will realize a return) will do so because of the quality of character instilled by the founder. That principle holds true regardless of how many zeros are in your company valuation. The ultimate fate of the company often finds its beginning in the character of the founder. You are a reading this book because you are on the other end of that spectrum. Your character has laid the foundation for a company that has demonstrable value and which has the potential to benefit your family and your successors for generations to come.

If you are like most successful family business owners, your goals in the succession planning process are two-fold:

1). Emerge out the other side with confidence that you will have enough money to live the kind of life you want for as long as you live without having to go back to work, rely on government benefits or depend on your children for your daily bread.

2). See the next generation of ownership fully equipped to continue serving the customers, clients and employees you care about with excellence and continue building on the foundation you started.

Before either of those objectives can be met, they must be fully defined by the only person qualified to give them meaning – you, the founder.

The founder must provide the answers to very personal, non-technical questions like:

- What kind of lifestyle do we want to enjoy going forward?

- What does our family history tell us about how long we think we'll live?

- Which clients, customers and employees are we most concerned about in this transition? Why? How do we prepare them?

- Who do we feel is qualified to run the organization going forward? Where are they on the continuum of preparedness?

- What past experience and character qualities would give us confidence that our successor is prepared to run the organization without our ongoing involvement?

- What elements of our company culture are most important to our customers and clients? How have we memorialized them in the company?

- What are the core values that have enabled our company to thrive?

- What are the key indicators that our children are prepared to run the organization?

The answers to these questions (and others like them) give context to the strategies and tactics that need to be evaluated when crafting an exit strategy. The founder also is responsible for defining and reinforcing the culture of the business. Language is a critical element of a business' culture. That is why one of the other key roles the founder plays is creating a common language used within the business.

We also need a common language for the purposes of this book. Fear not. I promised this was not a technical book. Instead, I'm going to introduce you in the next chapter to the foundational language of succession planning so you can begin putting words behind your vision for the next phase of your business.

Chapter 2: Talking The Talk

As promised, I will avoid using industry jargon whenever possible but you will see a few terms used frequently throughout. I'll define them briefly here to help ensure we're linking the same ideas to the same words. As you proceed in your journey of succession planning, it may be helpful to begin building a glossary of key terms used in your own business as a reference and a resource for your successors as well!

Founder – The founder can refer to the single person who first formed the company, it could be a group of founding individuals or it can just generally refer to the current generation of ownership. That means it could be the third generation of owners for the business who are now looking to plan a transition to the fourth generation. For purposes of this book, I will still refer to the current generation as the founder. The main thing is I am talking about the current owners who are making decisions about the company's future.

Emergency Plan – The emergency plan is a written set of instructions regarding what needs to happen for the company to continue operating in the event one or more of the current owners dies or otherwise leaves the company unexpectedly. It is *NOT* the same thing as key man insurance. Key man insurance is a tool used in the emergency plan. It is not the plan itself. You can have $100M of key man life insurance and still have your company implode in the wake of your death.

Exit Strategy – The exit strategy is one part of the long-term succession plan and covers a specific phase within that plan. It details the specific tactics, mechanisms and strategies that will allow the founder to remove him or herself from the ownership and operations of the business. The exit strategy is fully executed when the founder is sufficiently removed that their approval and presence is no longer required for the day-to-day management of the business. If it can run whether you (ever) show up or not, you've completed your exit strategy.

Succession Plan/Planning – The succession plan is the compilation of instructions, plans, strategies and tactics for preparing the next generation of owners to lead an organization.

Exit Planning – I use this term interchangeably with Succession Planning throughout the book. It's a more generic term for the process of leaving your business in an orderly, efficient manner.

Key Man – Key man is a financial services & legal term referring to a value-critical employee in the company. I realize it's not "PC" these days to use a gender specific term to explain a concept that includes both men and women. I didn't make up the term and I don't know what would be more palatable. Key human? Key biped? It may change in the future but this is what we're stuck with until the industry comes up with something different.

Success Team – The success team is the group of advisors and professionals responsible for supporting the founder while he or she executes the emergency plan, exit strategy and succession plan. It's important to note that they do not execute these plans *FOR* the founder. They play a supporting role throughout the process but the founder's involvement, action and leadership is critical.

Wealth – This one is more complicated to define than it seems at face value. The question of how you define wealth for your family is one that must be answered *as a family.* But watch out! Limiting your definition to just the business itself, the portfolio of stocks, bonds and cash or even the totality of your financial assets may not produce the result you desire. For the purposes of this book, let's assume your wealth includes the totality of your financial resources, your key relationships and connections and your family history. That broad definition will help shed light on why each member of your success team (described in a later chapter) is necessary for a successful transfer of wealth.

Those are the main terms you need to be familiar with for the purposes of this book. There are many other technical terms you might hear an attorney, tax professional or financial planner use when describing different strategies used in a succession plan. Don't allow yourself to be intimidated by all the jargon.

If you don't understand the fundamentals of your specific strategy, raise your hand and make your advisor explain it in layperson terms. If he or she can't do that, they're probably not the right person for your team. Remember: Your job is not to become an expert in succession planning and you shouldn't need a technical dictionary to have a conversation with your advisor. The things you need to be an expert on are you, your family, your business and the goals you have for each one.

A final word about gender specific language in the book: I use many examples throughout the book of clients who have built successful businesses. There are some stories of female founders and some of male founders. I realize there continues to be an overrepresentation of men in the world of business leadership and it's a sensitive issue for many. I use general pronouns like him, her, he, and she throughout the book and in the interviews in Part III.

Please don't take offense if you feel one pronoun happens to be used more than another. It's not intentional and I have done my best to pull examples equally of both successful men and women. I've got two daughters and expect them to be powerful, successful women in their future endeavors. That being said, let's move on so I can help you differentiate between the real succession planning your family needs and the many counterfeits in the marketplace today.

Chapter 3: Spotting the Real Thing

What would you do if someone offered the paper above as payment for your services? Would you accept it as legal tender? Unless it was from your eight-year-old grandson playing "store", you'd probably tell the person to go suck an egg. You would never accept such an obvious fake in your own business. Yet, when it comes to exit and succession planning, many people are duped into thinking they have a plan just because they were sold some key man insurance, have a buy-sell agreement or an advisor told them they "do succession planning".

There's an anecdote about U.S. Secret Service agents learning to identify counterfeit money by studying only real dollar bills. They know its feel by focusing on its weight, its texture and its density. They know how it smells and how it interacts with different kinds of light. They probably even have to taste it! There's no reason for them to spend time studying the thousands of fakes out there because they are so intimately familiar with the real thing. So it is with succession planning.

The three tests for determining whether you're getting the real thing are as follows:

Succession planning is…

- ✓ a distinct professional discipline practiced by a specialist in that field;

- ✓ a service in itself and;

- ✓ process-oriented rather than product-oriented.

Succession/exit planning is still in its infancy as a distinct industry and the financial services world is replete with counterfeits. There are still many practitioners promoting a single product as a self-completing succession plan. These succession planning "strategies" are usually nothing more than thinly veiled sales tools designed to sell life insurance. However, claiming life insurance is a succession plan is kind of like saying the cab ride from the airport to your hotel was the vacation. It's an important part of the process to be sure but it's not the whole thing.

The succession planning process is divided into four parts:

1. A personal wealth management plan for you & your family

2. An operational assessment & valuation of your business

3. A detailed transition plan

4. Post-transition coaching

Several organizations have developed proprietary processes for their clients and they range in length from a six-step process out to as many as twenty-two individual steps. You will find that every company who is doing real succession planning will be able to fit their process into this four-part framework regardless of many steps they choose to split it into for marketing purposes.

Part 1: The Personal Wealth Management Plan

The personal wealth management plan sets the foundation for the rest of the process because it helps you get clear on your current financial position as well as what financial resources you need to sustain your lifestyle indefinitely in the future. The plan also helps identify any gaps in your risk management picture (such as the potential for an unexpected medical event to cause a personal financial crisis) and define how much variation you and your spouse are willing to accept month to month in your income. I call that your "sleep at night factor". In other words, what level of month-to-month decline in your investment portfolio will cause you to start losing sleep? That is your true risk tolerance.

A complete wealth management plan should leave you with a clear pathway to achieving your goals in the following areas:

- Clarifying your vision for the future

- Harmonizing your work & life balance

- Creating financial comfort for your family

- Protecting your family & your resources

- Establishing your legacy

The personal wealth management plan should also draw out your core values and beliefs. It is critical for your team of advisors to clearly understand what is most important to you in terms of your goals for the next part of your life and ***why*** those goals are important to you. Life is dynamic and conditions will change. Having a deep belief in why you are pursuing certain goals will help you stay the course during challenging circumstances.

This portion of your personal wealth management plan (the values and beliefs part) provides a stable foundation for evaluating potential strategies throughout the rest of the succession planning process. For instance, if your #1 core value is generosity toward others in recognition of all that God has given you, it seems likely that your advisory team ought to integrate philanthropic planning into the exit strategy. However, if your #1 core value is teaching self-reliance and hard work, a gifting strategy may not be the right fit for you. There are so many tactics and strategies available in the exit planning process, it is important to have a sense of what is important to you so your team can craft a plan that is in alignment with your values.

Part 2: The Operational Assessment & Valuation

The second part of the exit planning process is the operational assessment for your business. I sometimes also refer to this as the opportunity assessment because so much of the analysis involves identifying opportunities to enhance and protect the value of your business. The idea is to have the members of your advisory team help you evaluate your company from an outsider's perspective. I will go into more detail about the differences between how a buyer sees a business versus how the seller sees it in a later chapter.

The operational assessment should cover at least the following components:

- Review the historical financial statements for clarity and compliance

- Review the corporate structure and legal documents

- Update employee handbooks and identify/quantify any outstanding employee issues and liabilities

- Establish an valuation trend via a formal or informal valuation (ideally you want at least three years of historical data)

- Assess which components of the business are for sale vs. which will be retained by the current owners

- Review executive compensation structure including tax-qualified retirement plans and/or unfunded liabilities under any existing deferred compensation plans

- Identify value-critical processes, products and people

- Identify opportunities for enhancing the value of the business prior to a transition

- Clarify value proposition for a potential successor

- Develop a written emergency plan for your business in the interim in case your long term plans aren't realized

- Assess any existing life insurance policies and complete a needs analysis including pre-underwriting for any potential insureds

- Check any supplier, vendor, and client contracts as well as covenants for existing financing agreements to identify the implications of a change in ownership

- Assess the potential tax consequences for all stakeholders under an asset sale scenario versus a stock sale scenario

- Meet with a charitable giving professional to identify any pre-sale giving opportunities to accomplish philanthropic goals and reduce the tax-impact of a sale

Completing an operational assessment prior to sitting down with a potential buyer or successor helps to identify existing issues before they become deal killers. The operational assessment should be completed in collaboration with multiple specialists including a business consultant, planned giving specialists, a tax professional, estate planning attorney and business attorney.

This part of the process can take anywhere from 3 months to several years depending on the issues uncovered and the opportunities identified. Remember that, all else being equal, the amount of tax a business owner will pay during a sale will be inversely related to the length of the transition. In other words, an emergency sale situation in which the owner simply has to get out immediately will usually result in a higher tax liability than a scenario where an owner has several years to plan prior to exiting the business.

Part 3: The Transition Plan

The third part of a succession plan is the Transition Plan itself. It's at this point that your advisors will take the information gathered in your personal financial plan and the operational assessment and use it to develop the specific tactics and strategies to move you from where you are to where you want to be. It's during this part of the plan where negotiations begin, legal documents are signed, financing arrangements are made, money changes hands and the plan moves forward.

The Transition Plan portion of the process requires close collaboration between the members of your success team, especially your financial planner, your tax professional and your legal professionals. I typically suggest at least a monthly conference call with these members of the team to keep each party up to date on the most current information.

This stage can feel a bit like a "hurry up and wait" scenario since certain portions of the process will be dependent on other people to be completed. For example, negotiations over the final purchase agreement can take weeks or even months to complete as the buyer's attorneys and forensic accountants review all of your documents. A final timeline will be outside of your control so its important to set appropriate expectations for how many rounds of back and forth may be involved. Don't get frustrated. Provide the requested information and keep the relationship cordial albeit at arms length if possible. The Transition Plan bridges the gap between hypothetical and the reality.

A final note on Part III: It is critical that any estate or philanthropic strategies you intend to incorporate into your plan are implemented <u>before</u> you execute the transition to your successor/buyer. Think of your transition plan as having a big red button that says, "LAUNCH" on it. Once you push the button, it can sometimes be impossible to go back. Make sure your success team conducts a final safety check before liftoff.

Part 4: Post Transition Coaching

Part four of the succession planning process is the post-transition follow through. Assuming you have successfully made it through parts 1 – 3 and your deal has gone through, you now have the challenge of following through on everything you said you would do in the purchase agreement. Many deals involving a sale to an outside buyer will require the seller to stay on board for a period of time to help the new owners.

It's not uncommon for a purchase agreement to make a percentage of the final sales price contingent upon the exiting owner helping the new owner achieve certain goals. The agreement may have a tiered payout structure based on realizing certain client retention rates, achieving new sales or closing the existing business in the sales pipeline. You need to be clear on what is expected of you and what goals you need to hit in order to maximize your net proceeds following the transition of your business.

In addition to everything else you'll have going on once your deal has been executed, you may also find yourself in an unfamiliar role of either being a non-owner employee or even a retiree. This may be the first time in your life you have had to follow someone else's rules in "your" business! This is where the planning process comes full circle and why it is so critical that you invested time months earlier in Part 1 on your personal wealth management plan.

Your personal wealth management plan should have included a retirement lifestyle plan to help you clearly articulate and visualize how you would spend your time, what you would do, how you would stay healthy and what things you wanted to learn once you no longer had to go to the office each day. You may be wondering, "Why is that so important? I thought retirement was supposed to make life easier.". Not so fast, Jack!

The truth is the transition into retirement is stressful! So stressful, in fact, that researchers at the University of Michigan have determined a person's likelihood of experiencing a heart attack _increases 40%_ in the 12 months following retirement from work[2]. Retirement

---

[2] Moon JR1, Glymour MM, Subramanian SV, Avendaño M, Kawachi I. (2012). *Transition to retirement and risk of cardiovascular disease: prospective*

21

is ranked #10 out of 43 events listed on the American Institute of Stress' list of life's most stressful events. Believe me – you need a plan for transitioning into retirement. Your life may depend on it!

The post-transition plan is also when you get to go back to your personal wealth management plan and start checking things off your bucket list. Did you want to buy that car you've wanted since high school as a celebration? Go do it (after you talk to your financial planner to make sure it fits into your lifetime income plan of course). Has your wife always wanted to go to Italy? Take her there. Was it your goal to finish your college degree or maybe get your Masters degree? Start your applications.

Realizing your life's goals requires you to take consistent action just the way growing a successful business required consistent action. The post-transition follow through portion of your plan is the key to increasing your personal satisfaction with life. It is your happiness roadmap. You will have just recently come through a major life change and your world may look surprisingly foreign. Without it that road map, you're more likely to experience regret, depression and anxiety rather than the peace and fulfillment you hoped would be on the other side of the storm.

analysis of the US health and retirement study. Soc Sci Med. 2012 Aug;75(3):526-30. doi: 10.1016/j.socscimed.2012.04.004.

There are many different frameworks that can be laid on top of this four-part chassis but they'll all have the same basic components. The key is your advisory team needs to follow a consistent process for planning your exit rather than simply "shooting from the hip" or, worse yet, selling you on an insurance product, investment vehicle or a single strategy and declaring you healed.

What Is This Stuff Worth?

You have probably figured out by now that succession planning is time intensive and requires specialized expertise. A natural question that follows is, "If this is a separate service, how much does this service cost?". I have seen many different pricing models including hourly fees, flat rate programs, retainers and sliding scales based on the value of the business. I believe the cost of the planning should be linked to several factors including:

- the timeframe for completing the transition

- the number of owners involved

- the scale of the businesses being transitioned (i.e. how many entities, what kind of assets do they hold, etc.)

- the type of transition being targeted (i.e. which of The Three Doors you're going through as described later)

- the number of employees at the company

- the revenue of the company

It's a very different scope of work to help a franchisee sell two franchises than it is to help a $50M manufacturing business with 100 employees and a national distribution network transition to the third generation. That becomes even more work when the next generation consists of three kids who each want to be involved in the day-to-day operations and who don't get along. There can be huge variations in the amount of time involved so the compensation structure for the advisory team needs to have sufficient flexibility to accommodate these variances.

In my experience, the most fair and flexible structure consists of a combination of an up-front planning fee covering Parts 1 and 2 (the personal wealth management plan and the operational assessment) plus a retainer on a sliding scale to develop and oversee Parts 3 and 4 (the Transition Plan and the post-transition follow through coaching). The flat fee portion can range from $5,000 on the low end up to $100,000 on the high end (sometimes beyond for extremely complex plans with multiple owners) while the sliding scale can range from 0.15% - 1.00% of the organization's adjusted EBITDA[3] or another earnings-centric formula.

Even the term "organization" can be subject to interpretation. You and your advisor need to define

---

[3] EBITDA is an accounting metric, which stands for Earnings Before Interest, Taxes, Depreciation and Amortization.

which entities are covered under the planning agreement as well as which owners and/or families are covered. I consider the organization as one client (which includes all sub-entities/assets of the holding company if one exists) and each family as a client in my own practice. Each client is covered under a separate planning agreement. Your advisor may be setup differently but the point is you need to be clear about what's included, who the client is, what the scope of each agreement is and how the various elements of the process are compensated.

Another variable to consider is how any commissions from the sale of life insurance products will affect the fees you pay. This is another point of variation from advisor to advisor. Some advisors choose to offset the planning fees with the insurance commissions received while others consider them separate services to be compensated separately. Still others may choose to forego commissions from life insurance entirely by either working with a trusted insurance professional who would receive the commissions instead.

There's not necessarily a right answer. It comes down to what you are comfortable with and what you've agreed on with your advisor. The one thing your advisor CANNOT do is rebate the insurance commissions back to you. Rebating is when the insurance professional gives their commission back to the person who bought the insurance. It is illegal and it should be a major red flag if your advisor even mentions this as an option.

In my opinion, I am least comfortable with the commission-only model in which an adviser or (or any professional) doesn't quote a total fee up front but says the cost of the planning will be 100% covered by insurance commissions. My questions in that case are:

1). How do you know the client is going to need new life insurance as part of their plan at all?;

2). How do you know what your commission is going to be before you even start planning? And;

3). All else being equal, what is your process for determining which insurance carriers, products & styles are in your client's best interest other than which one pays the highest commission?

Again, this is 100% my opinion but I feel there is more potential for abuse and an incentive for an advisor to be product-driven under a commission-only model. It increases the incentive to sell a product in order to make sure he or she gets sufficiently compensated for the intense planning work it takes to do succession planning right. Whichever compensation model your advisor uses, it's critical they disclose what they expect the total cost to be up-front as well as disclose all sources of compensation they will receive throughout the process whether its directly from you or from other sources.

Chapter 4: The Three Doors Out Of Your Business

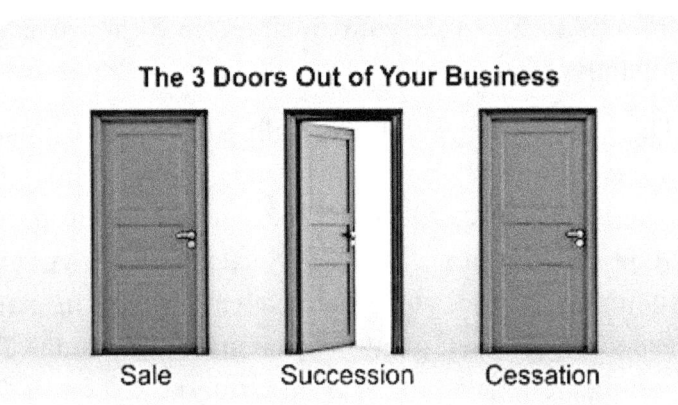

The 3 Doors Out of Your Business

Sale — Succession — Cessation

Many business owners feel overwhelmed when faced with the complexities of exiting their business. One of the ways you can increase your likelihood of making a successful transition is by narrowing down your options. That's actually easier than it sounds because there are only three exits out of any business.

No matter what industry, sector or size, the options for exiting your business are the same. The details of your specific transition may be different as a result of the nuances of your particular business but you will ultimately leave via one of these exits. I call them The Three Doors.

Door #1 - The Sale Door. The Sale Door means a sale to an outside buyer or group of buyers. This is the classic scenario most founders think of when they imagine someone writing them a check, exchanging keys and walking away. The outside buyer may be a competitor, a private equity group or anybody else who is not already working in your business and intends to integrate your business into their existing business or portfolio.

The Sale Door will typically have the highest immediate cash payout for the founder but that comes at a price in both time and stress. Preparing your business for a successful sale can take years of planning before you ever have a buyer in hand, especially if you want to maximize its value. The average length of a sale transaction in 2015 was 7 – 10 months[4]. That means the owners were trying to keep their business running at peak performance, negotiate a sale and (quietly) prepare to exit for 7 – 10 months. Ask anyone who has gone through it and they will tell you it was one of the most stressful times of their life. Make sure you're healthy enough, you're mentally/emotionally prepared and your spouse is on board if you are thinking the Sale Door is right for you.

Sale strategies tend to focus on the following characteristics:

- System building

- Documentation of value-critical processes, personnel & property

---

[4] Everett, Craig R., Ph.D, *2015 Capital Markets Report.* Pepperdine University, Malibu, California. Online: http://bschool.pepperdine.edu/about/people/faculty/appliedresearch/researc h/pcmsurvey/content/ppcm-report-2015.pdf

- Developing incentive plans to retain key personnel

- Team building within the organization

- Intellectual property development

- KPI management

- Establishing a long term valuation trend

- Public relations management

- Information management

Door #2 - The Succession Door. Succession involves finding someone already working in the business to transition ownership to. It can be a family member or a non-family member like a key employee or a management team. The transition can be done over time or in a lump sum buyout. The key is the successor is someone already working in the company who plans to continue its operations. This may also mean looking for a new employee or partner to bring into the business to eventually transition it to.

The Succession Door will often have a lower up-front cash payout for the founder but can have the highest total value when estate tax savings, loan interest and any ongoing consulting fees are factored in. The founder may need to be prepared to finance some of the purchase agreement (i.e. accept a note receivable) from the successor as well. That means they will also probably need significant outside assets to fall back and to ensure they are not financially ruined if the succession plan does not go as expected. The expected timeline for a founder exiting via the Succession Door is generally a minimum of 2 years with 5 – 7 years being more typical.

Succession strategies tend to emphasize:

- Family dynamics coaching (for family transfers)

- Estate plan integration

- Insurance & risk management planning

- Wealth transfer vehicles (installment note, life insurance policy, ongoing payroll, etc.)

- Restricted stock plans or stock bonus arrangements

- Buy-sell planning for employee transfers

- Possibly working with Third Party Administrator & financing team for an Employee Stock Ownership Plan (ESOP)

- Definitely working with estate planning attorney & tax advisory team

Door #3 - The Cessation Door. Cessation means you simply cease (or stop) doing business. You would potentially sell the company's hard assets (if any exist), collect your accounts receivable over a few months and go home. It could also be a more gradual winding down by referring clients to another trusted professional over time.

Cessation does not mean bankruptcy (although that is one way operations can quickly cease). In this case, Cessation means a founder has built substantial pools of assets outside the business such that they don't actually have to sell or transition it to another person to achieve their financial goals. They can simply pick a date to close the doors and walk away (or retire). The Cessation Door is about achieving total control over your retirement. It can take years to get there so be prepared.

I work with these clients to create what's called an I.L.T. portfolio. The "I" stands for Income Streams. We focus on first creating at least three independent income streams to meet their core spending needs. The "L" stands for Liquid Capital. This is their opportunity war chest. It is a pot of funds set aside to quickly capitalize on real estate, business or other investment opportunities that arise. The "T" stands for Tax-advantaged Assets. This is where we utilize estate-planning tools (such as certain irrevocable trusts) and qualified retirement plans to create tax-advantaged pools of assets for the current and future generations. This approach is for families who are looking to achieve complete financial independence and it dovetails perfectly with the Cessation Door.

Cessation strategies tend to emphasize:

- Transferring value out of the business over time to build up a tax-efficient income stream that will outlive the business

- Accumulating assets in tax-advantaged savings vehicles and non-tax qualified accounts

- Developing multiple streams of income

- Developing a rental or investment real estate portfolio

- Achieving financial independence

- Building assets outside the business

- Investing in other businesses

- Developing an internal team to run your businesses for you

Every business exit strategy will fit into one of those three options no matter how complex the final details end up being. With approximately 33% of businesses for sale in 2015 failing to transact[5], it is critical to identify beforehand which exit best matches your circumstances and goals. For example, it may be that a founder ideally would like to exit through the Sale Door but, upon further analysis, his success team determines his business isn't sufficiently systematized to allow an external buyer to easily

---

[5] Everett, Craig R., Ph.D, *2015 Capital Markets Report.* Pepperdine University, Malibu, California. Online: http://bschool.pepperdine.edu/about/people/faculty/appliedresearch/researc h/pcmsurvey/content/ppcm-report-2015.pdf

operate it without him. In that case, the founder has two options.

First, he can continue pursuing the Sale strategy by extending his exit timeline and focusing on building systems internally to make the business more transferable. Second, he can decide to pursue an exit via the Succession or Cessation doors depending on which is a better match given his current constraints. Either way, he only has to make one decision at a time and he has a clear pathway for how to eventually accomplish his goal. Breaking your ultimate goal down into bite-sized chunks is the key to getting from where you are to where you want to be.

It is also important for a founder to consider their desire for personal recognition and legacy in addition to the business' financial and operational circumstances when evaluating the exit options. As I wrote previously, the sale door often will have the highest immediate cash payout for the founder but this potentially comes at a cost of lower legacy satisfaction in many cases. The buyer may want to remove the personal touches the founder made to the business. She may want to incorporate the company into her existing branding and eliminate the old brand entirely. She may terminate most of the employees you labored side by side with for so many years.

In contrast, a succession strategy typically will have a higher legacy satisfaction rating for the founder because his name, character and the culture he instilled in the company will likely live on in his chosen successor(s). In a cessation strategy, founders can sometimes be left feeling as though they failed simply because the business no longer exists. I emphasize how a cessation strategy is really about achieving absolute financial independence and control, which is something to celebrate. In all cases, the founder needs to be aware of how those changes may impact his sense of personal satisfaction after the close of the deal.

Up to this point, we've covered some basic terminology, I've given you the tools for differentiating between real succession planning and the many counterfeits out there and we have identified the options for making your exit. The next chapter lays out ten principles to keep in mind as you approach your own exit planning journey before moving into Part II of the book.

Chapter 5: Ten Principles To Avoid A Failed Succession Plan

Failure can provide a better education than the top MBA program. I certainly feel I've gotten my money's worth from my own various failures over the years. The benefit is I've been able to learn from them, move forward and had the opportunity to help many business owners better navigate their own transitions as a result.

I devote considerable time in Part II to what I call the Five Big Flubs of Succession Planning. Think of these as the Hall of Fame categories of succession plan failures. They are the repeat offenders. However, there were also a few key foundational business lessons I've compiled which I felt compelled to include here as well. Each of these has implications for going businesses as well as those about to enter a transition period. Here they are in rapid-fire succession:

1. Always have a Plan B.

Having an alternative route to your destination gives you margin for error. You will face challenges in executing any transition. Fear will creep in at times and it can be paralyzing. When that happens, ask yourself, "What will I do if this doesn't work out?". Write your answer down so you can see there is a viable Plan B.

Another way to ask the question is, "What's the realistic worst case scenario if our plan doesn't work? Is that acceptable?". It's counterintuitive but having a Plan B to reassure yourself in times of fear is a powerful tool. It will free you to take action and actually make Plan A more likely to succeed.

2. The inside always comes out.

In Psalm 55:20-21 in the Bible, King David tells of a friend who betrayed him during a time of trouble. He states, "As for my companion, he betrayed his friends; he broke his promises. His words are as smooth as butter, but in his heart is war. His words are as soothing as lotion, but underneath are daggers!"[6]

Every relationship has its honeymoon phase during which all parties are on their best behavior. Unfortunately, the happy faces only last so long. I discovered that a person's true character almost always comes to the surface in times of stress or trouble. Negotiations and business transitions are inherently stressful endeavors. Be prepared to learn a lot about yourself and the person across the table in the process. Make sure the real version is someone you want to do business with.

3. Cash may be king, but patience is Parliament.

There are many types of leverage a person can bring to the negotiating table in order to obtain a more

---

[6] *Holy Bible,* New Living Translation, copyright © 1996, 2004, 2015 by Tyndale House Foundation.

favorable deal. Cash is usually the most powerful since most sellers are willing to take less than full price if they receive payment up front. However, I've seen patience is where the real power lies. It's often said in negotiations, "Whoever talks first, loses". The ability to be patient in deal-making means the buyer or seller can put the burden on the other person to make the first concession.

4. Work the negative.

I had the opportunity to purchase a company I worked for years ago. I was flattered to be approached by the owner and intrigued by the idea of becoming my own boss. However, I discovered not everyone was as enthusiastic as I was about becoming the successor in the firm I worked at years ago.

As it turned out, there had been several previous attempts to identify a successor before me. All had failed. Each potential successor or acquirer had fled – literally refused to return phone calls – from the seller once they discovered what was going on behind the scenes in the business.

There were also people in my own life that tried to warn me things weren't what they seemed and this wasn't a business (or a person) I should be involved with. I recognize now that I knew it too in my heart. The truth is I so enjoyed having my ego stroked being the "chosen one" that I suppressed that negative feedback.

That's why it is so important to surround yourself with advisors who care about you enough they'll do whatever it takes to get your attention when its important. Seek out people who have a viewpoint and professional background that's different than yours. Be brutally honest with yourself. Welcome negative feedback and use it to make better decisions.

5.   Partners usually aren't.

There was another employee at a company I worked for years ago whom I was considering becoming partners with in buying out the company founder. We had worked together for several years and I thought it would be helpful to have a partner to mitigate some of the costs and share the load of business development. I also assumed he was a good choice because we were friends.

I asked for feedback on the idea of including my friend as a partner during a planning session I attended with a group of trusted business leaders. One CEO asked me, "What does this person bring to the table that you either can't do yourself or can't hire someone else to do without giving up control?". I rattled off my reasoning about being friends and the opportunity to lower my risk by sharing expenses, etc. Their advice came back unanimous – DON'T DO IT!

Nearly every CEO at that table had their own personal stories about business partnerships with friends that went wrong. It didn't matter that they had been best friends before going into business together. It was usually even worse when the partner was a spouse.

Many partnerships come about as a result of friendship, convenience or just not wanting to hurt someone's feelings rather than sound business reasons. In almost every case, the result is one person working more hours, generating more of the revenue and handling more of the responsibilities than the other person. Those factors often wind up creating an undercurrent of jealousy, bitterness and resentment. Very rarely will you find partners whose respective skills complement each other to such an extent that it justifies the existential threat posed by the partnership itself.

The potential partnership I mentioned I was considering never even got off the ground (thankfully). The process of trying to buy that founder out was so dysfunctional that it ended with me leaving the company to start my own firm 10 months later. The aftermath of my departure from that company showed me just how big of a mistake it would have been to become business partners with my friend. There were ongoing strings of vitriolic emails for months, hours spent with attorneys, several threatened lawsuits and irreparable damage done to relationships with several major clients who were caught in the middle. It also wound up destroying my relationship with a guy who I considered a close friend.

My advice on partnerships (especially with a spouse or a close friend) now mirrors that of my CEO companions on that day around the conference table – DON'T DO IT! There has to be an undeniable complement of mutually exclusive skill sets between the partners and Ph.D. level self-awareness on the part of the partners for it to even have a chance of working out. This successful combination is so astoundingly rare that Hollywood makes movies about the ones that work out. There are so many other options available for engaging the skills of a key employee long term without giving up ownership. There is almost always a better option than going into an equity partnership.

6. Pray but verify.

I believe there are many sincere people of faith who are committed to living out their beliefs in their business. I am including this point not to make light of what they are doing or to undermine their motivations. However, I also know from experience there are just as many business people who stick a "Jesus fish" (or whatever other religious logo suits their fancy) on their business card in order to curry favor with a niche market. If working with someone who shares your spiritual convictions is important to you, my advice in this area is two-fold. First, don't make a decision to do business with someone simply based on flowery spiritual language or Bible verses in a brochure.

Proverbs 20:11 states, "Even children are known by the way they act, whether their conduct is pure, and whether it is right.". Watch their actions, talk to their friends and staff to find tangible evidence of their faith actually having an impact in their life. If faith in business is important to you, the question isn't "does this person believe what I believe?". Instead, the question to answer is "does this person's track record of behavior match what they are saying they believe?".

When you do encounter the inevitable religious poser along the way (because we all will eventually), don't let a negative encounter tarnish or diminish your own convictions. This was the situation I found myself in during the business transaction I described earlier. My encounter with such rank religious hypocrisy almost resulted in me walking away from my own faith completely.

However, what I've learned since is a person's actions are really just an indication of the condition of their own heart as an individual rather than a reflection of the validity of the belief system they claim to subscribe to. It's not easy but the best course of action is to forgive them, release it and move on.

   7. Know when to say "No".

I worked at another company where they held bi-weekly "management meetings". You may be familiar with this phenomenon in your own company. They were supposed to be progress reports and strategic planning sessions. In actuality, the meetings were an opportunity for the owners to spend 90-minutes brain-dumping whatever marketing ideas, projects, general gripes or research topics that had come across their desk in the last two weeks onto the CFO and I.

As Chief Operating Officer, I would walk out of every meeting with a headache and a list of new projects that "absolutely had to be addressed" before the next meeting. There was no evaluation of which projects to undertake first and no consideration as to the necessity of having an immediate answer to the questions. There was also no master plan from the CEO that gave context as to how any of these critical projects fit in with the larger mission.

Everything was considered urgent and important because there was no leader setting a vision and keeping the ship on course. Occasionally, something would trigger a reminder months later and an angry tirade would arrive in my inbox demanding to know why an idea wasn't followed up on and lambasting the lack of accountability in the company. Sound familiar?

There are only so many hours in a day and only so much mental energy available. Founders have to prioritize and evaluate the things they devote their energy to throughout the course of the day. That kind of focused leadership sets the priorities for everyone else in the organization. Focused leadership also means being willing to say, "No" to things. Sometimes it means worthy projects will get set aside or delayed indefinitely simply because they aren't the best use of anyone's time. Perhaps lower value projects can or should be delegated.

Be ruthless in your evaluation of what deserves time and attention from you and your direct reports. Keep your priorities in front of you at all times. I suggest using a format like Stephen Covey's Time Management Matrix to prioritize your to-do's once the vision has been cast.

8. Wear your walking shoes to the negotiating table.

I was so caught up in the ego of being the chosen successor in the firm I mentioned earlier that I ignored the warnings all around me. I so badly craved the validation I was getting from the process that I couldn't let go even when I knew it was the right thing to do. I'm not alone in making that mistake.

I was doing some consulting with a woman who was considering purchasing an existing business. The sellers had been running the operation as a side business in addition to their day jobs. That isn't necessarily a problem but this business was in a highly scrutinized, highly regulated industry in which deviation from even the smallest letter of law could result in high penalties or even a complete shut down of the business following an inspection.

My client mentioned the current owners were being evasive in answering specific questions about the business (strike one), weren't forthcoming in providing the documentation she requested (strike two) and refused to get an independent appraisal to back up their asking price (strike three). The answer in this situation was obvious from my chair. She needed to provide a list of must-have information and a date for providing it if the negotiations were to proceed. She also needed to be willing to walk away if the sellers refused to meet her requirements.

Emotional attachment equally affects sellers and buyers in a business transaction. I also see it frequently with people who get attached to a particular stock in their investment portfolio. They hold onto a stock position far longer or own more of it than prudence would dictate because they are emotionally attached to the investment. The remedy in all cases is to look to your team of advisors (your success team) to help you detach emotionally from the transaction. Your success team gets paid to keep you safe and tell you the truth even when it's not what you want to hear. They will help you know when something isn't right. Take their counsel and be ready to walk away.

9. Believe in your value.

As you approach the negotiating table in your business transition, pause a moment to reaffirm your value as an individual and the value of your business. I'm not talking about demanding six times the market value of the company. I'm referring to a quiet self-assurance that you are who you say you are, you are a person of value, you can create value for other people and people need what you offer. It's not about ego. It's about confidence.

Use tools like positive affirmations and journaling your successes to help you move forward from a solid foundation of quiet confidence if you struggle in this area. Having a healthy foundation of confidence in your value increases the chances you will come away with a deal where everyone wins and reduces your susceptibility to the Four Delusions (discussed later).

10. Don't be an @#&!^(_$%.

There are some people who still believe hardball tactics are the only way to get ahead in business. I call them "Takers". Their goal is to get as much out of the other person as possible and give as little as possible in return. They treat every little negotiation like they're a conquering general and they end up with deals that are as effective as the Treaty of Versailles.

Just because you are sitting on opposite sides of the negotiating table doesn't mean you are enemies. That table should be thought of as a place where the parties are coming together to brainstorm solutions to one another's problems. You are there to help each other. There is no reason to treat the other person as though they're stupid, like they have nothing to offer or as though they should be grateful just to be in your presence. You both have problems. You both have good ideas.

Why not start with the belief that the other person is as good-natured as you are and has your best interest at heart? Let them prove otherwise. As I mentioned in #2 above, the real person always comes out eventually and you will have the opportunity to decide whether they're someone you want to move forward with or not. Basically, just don't be a... jerk.

You now have a framework to help you differentiate between real succession planning and the many counterfeits in the marketplace. You also have a few personal guidelines to keep in mind as you approach the process. The next section of the book is where you really need to pay attention.

Consider holding this book in one hand and a mirror in the other so you can ask yourself, "Is this me? Am I making these mistakes right now?". Answering honestly could save you millions of dollars when it comes time to sell or otherwise transition your business. Without further ado, I give you *The Five Big Flubs of Succession Planning.*

Part II: The Five Big Flubs of Succession Planning

Chapter 6: The First Big Flub - Not Getting An Independent Valuation

Imagine for a moment you are at the airport. You've already gone through security and you are sitting at your gate waiting to board. Suddenly, you remember warm, edible food has not been served on airplanes since 1983 and you should probably go buy a sandwich to hold you over.

You finally make it to the front of the line and the clerk promptly tells you the tuna fish sandwich you're holding costs $147.53. Once you recover your senses and get up off the floor, you tell the clerk there must be some mistake. Only a fool or a crook would claim a tuna fish sandwich is worth $147.53 and only a bigger fool (or a desperately hungry person) would pay that much! There has to be a mistake.

"No mistake" says the clerk. "That's what it's worth.".

You calmly voice your concern saying, "How is that possible? Was the sandwich made from the last tuna on Earth? Will it give me crime-fighting powers? Did he owe you money? Tell me why I should pay $147.53.".

He responds, "Well, it took me a really long time to make this sandwich. I had to get up at 4:30 AM to get here, I had to learn how to work a can opener to access the tuna and I used electricity while toasting this delicious wheat bread. Then I had to open a jar of mayonnaise and expend more energy using the knife to spread it on the bread. It may have only taken me 14 minutes to make, but I've spent my entire life until this day preparing to make this sandwich! Plus, it is going to keep you hunger free for your entire flight! Besides that, I LOVE tuna fish and I know I would certainly pay that much if I were the one buying this sandwich. So that's what I think you should pay for it.".

You are not just trying to sell a tuna fish sandwich. You are attempting (or soon may be attempting) to sell a complex asset comprised of interwoven systems and long standing vendor and customer relationships founded on highly nuanced concepts such as trust and your personal reputation. My guess is you are also hoping to sell it for much more than $147.53. And yet, I've heard the following so many times it doesn't even surprise me anymore: "Oh, I know what my business is worth. I'm going to sell it for $ (<u>insert arbitrary number here</u>)".

When probed further as to how the he or she arrived at that value, the response often sounds like another version of the clerk's response above. "I've invested 30 years building this business. It's got unlimited growth potential for whoever buys it. Nobody makes widgets like we do.". Etc. Etc. Etc.

In one sense, your small business is an asset just like any other. There are revenues, expenses, profits (we hope) and losses. On the other hand, it is also a unique asset in that it there is not a readily available mechanism to establish a market value of the shares. This is because you own what is called a closely held business (i.e. the shares are held by a single person or a small group of owners). Its shares do not trade on an exchange and, therefore, there is not a reliable, fast way for the general public to put a market value on the business as a whole. Believe me, that's actually a good thing for you!

In contrast, the fair market value for shares of a publicly traded company is determined through a bidding process of buyers and sellers transacting thousands of times each day via the various public exchanges. This negotiating process occurs so frequently that up to the second market values are readily available for many of these companies.

We can generally assume that the market price for a publicly traded stock is fair at any given moment simply because:

a). No one is forcing buyers to purchase at a particular price nor are they forcing sellers to sell;

b). Buyers and sellers tend to act in their own best interest and, let's be honest, hardly anyone is so altruistic as to knowingly sell something to a complete stranger for less than they know it is worth;

c). There is typically a glut of publicly available information covering every aspect of those companies including past sales, new investments in technology, recently won contracts and a multitude of other data points and;

d). Buyers and sellers are constantly scrutinizing all available information to come up with what they consider to be the fair price to pay or receive for the shares.

The aforementioned factors mean the prices of publicly traded shares adjust almost instantaneously as new information becomes available about a company. Freely operating capital markets provide the best means we know of for determining fair market values for assets, which meet the above criteria (publicly traded assets).

Also important to note, owners of assets not fitting this criteria DO NOT possess a sustained competitive advantage over prospective buyers. In fact, they are legally not allowed to use information that is not publicly available to create an advantage for themselves. That is the definition of insider trading. It is illegal. If you think this is a point up for debate, just ask Martha Stewart how the U.S. Justice Department views the issue. This process, however, does NOT apply to private companies, most of which are small, closely held businesses just like yours.

The good news for you as an owner of such a business is you DO have a competitive advantage and you ARE allowed to use it! You know more about your business than anyone else in the world. You have secret information about what projects you are working on, what technology you are developing, the internal processes and techniques that make you so successful and you have a close network of relationships that can give you a leg up on the next contract. In that sense, you are the world's premier expert on your business.

Here's the bad news: The secret knowledge you possess about your business' past, present and future is not available to prospective buyers as they evaluate your business as a potential acquisition target. That means they have very limited ability to carry out due diligence as a buyer to come up with a fair market value. They are virtually 100% reliant on the information you provide to them to make their assessment.

Remember the guy selling the tuna fish sandwich? Don't be that guy. Every business owner who hopes to sell their business must have a credible means of proving to prospective buyers that their asking price is fair. One of the ways to establish such credibility is through an independent valuation. You put the negotiating power on your side of the table when you can tell your buyer, "You don't have to take my word for it. I believe so much in the value of this business that I asked someone else who doesn't even work here to go through all this private information about our company and determine the value.".

Having an independent appraisal removes the burden of proof from you and forces someone else to stake their reputation on the number they come up with. Many business transitions occur over time and require the buyer and the seller to work together. Giving your buyer a reason to doubt you from the very beginning is not a good way to get started with a positive, cooperative working relationship.

Not having third party verification gives your buyer an incentive to continue looking for proof that the business really IS NOT worth what you're asking even after the sale goes through. It's asking for trouble both now and later. The buyer gets mad, the lawyers get happy, the deal goes boom. You're not selling tuna fish. You're selling a business. Make sure you act like it.

Remedy #1: Prioritize obtaining an independent valuation.

Chapter 7: The First Big Flub Part deux - Not Getting an Independent Valuation Early Enough or Often Enough

You face a constantly changing economic and competitive landscape for your business. Seemingly insignificant factors can lead to large swings in value over a period of years. For instance, consider one business owner I met at a conference in Reno, NV several years ago.

The man and his wife owned a helicopter touring company based out of Hawaii. They started the company as a way to make supplemental income when he wasn't working as a pilot for the local fire department. When the movie Jurassic Park was released, their business started to boom. People wanted to see the famous waterfall from the opening scene.

Had this man and his wife gotten a valuation done for their business at that time, their growth projections would have reflected the recently increased consumer demand. Fast forward fifteen years and few people care about the film. Most of the ones who wanted to already have been to see the waterfall. The sudden demand caused by the film has subsided and the business revenue has returned to more historically normal levels.

The business may still be operating but its unlikely the temporary surge in demand would have been sustained. Therein lies the problem with a "one and done" valuation. A single data point does not provide a truly accurate picture of a business' long-term value. That brings us to the solution: establish a trend.

When it comes to your business, it's important to get your valuation done early and often. I know you're probably thinking, "We paid thousands of dollars to get our valuation done last time. I don't want to have to budget for that every few years!". It's true getting a frequent valuation used to be cost prohibitive. However, cloud technology and the Internet revolution has left no industry untouched. The valuation business has not been spared either.

We have the technology today that allows founders to obtain a market value for even a closely held business on a ***daily basis.*** There are probably exceptions out there if someone happens to own the only company in the world who has a specific government contract or if they have a complete corner on a market. Those are few and far between though and will most likely require the services of a specialist in that industry.

The other reason it is important to frequently value your business is because it allows your data to become seasoned as you establish a long-term value trend. Think of it from a buyer's prospective. How could you have any confidence that you were getting a reasonable deal if you had to make a decision based on a single data point for a company you didn't know existed a few months ago?

Unless you were buying a McDonald's franchise, there probably isn't another business just like the one you're interested in to compare the price against. What if the only data point was just conjured up yesterday? Worse yet, what if it was from six years ago?

If it were me buying that business, I would factor in a risk premium in the form of a deep discount off the asking price simply because I would have no idea where the current value sits in context with the company's historical value. Basing your asking price off a one-time valuation is like the old game show where they play a 1 second clip of a song and the contestant has to guess what it was. It's a pure shot in the dark.

Our brains use many short cuts to help us make decisions. One such shortcut is context. We evaluate information in relation to the information or environment around it. The more data points you can establish for the value of your business, the more context you give a potential buyer. This translates to more confidence on their part that you are serious about this transaction and there is real, sustained value in your business.

The earlier you can start building data points for your business value the better off you will be. This can give you an advantage when you go to sell as well as while you still own your business. The information required to determine a market value comes right from your balance sheet, your tax returns and your income statements (more on these later).

By establishing a value early on, you also can see how emphasizing different metrics (know as key performance indicators or "KPIs" for short) in the business can increase or decrease the value thereby helping you to develop a strategic growth plan.

Remedy #1b: Get Your Business Appraised Early and Often

Chapter 8: The Second Big Flub - Assuming The Buyer Views Your Company the Same Way You Do

My oldest daughter is seven years old at the time I'm writing this. She is beautiful, funny, smart and an absolute joy to be around (on most days). She has a great sense of humor and, in typical first child fashion, loves the spotlight. One of her favorite things to do is tell stories and jokes to entertain people.

She has developed some real zingers but she didn't quite have a handle on the logic of a properly formatted knock-knock joke when she was five. There was often absolutely no connection between the first part of the joke and the second. For example:

> *"Okay dad. Knock-knock"*
>
> *"Who's there?"*
>
> *"Hot dog"*
>
> *"Hot dog who?"*
>
> *"I ate a popsicle at lunch today and mom said I can't wear these shoes again because they make me trip."*

What was great was the joke still worked because she was five. The idiosyncrasy was funny in itself. We will need to have a different conversation if she is still doing it when she's thirty. The lesson here is a storyteller has a responsibility to communicate the concepts and ideas in a way ***their listener*** can understand and engage with.

Instead, what many inexperienced communicators do is arrange information in a format that makes sense to them. They often get frustrated when people don't interpret the data the same way. What they don't realize is the data only makes sense to them because they were there when the events behind the numbers occurred.

What the business owner sees as process consistency, the buyer can see as a failure to innovate. Where the owner sees staffing depth, the buyer sees bloated overhead. The owner sees tax efficiency; the buyer sees lack of consistent profits. The first thing taught in Communication 101 is this: It is ***the speaker's*** responsibility to communicate in a way the listener understands. It is not the listener's responsibility to read the speaker's mind. It's not the buyer's fault if they don't receive the information the way you intended. You're the one telling the story!

You are the world's foremost expert on your business. You understand the history, processes, growth potential secret recipes and customer relationships. That means you are not only the owner, you are also the storyteller in chief!

Any potential buyer has only the limited public information they are able to find on your business to form their opinions. Your job is to arrange the data about your business both in a way that represents what you know to be true but also so that it tells the story of the business in a way your buyer can understand and get excited about.

There are five essential tools available to tell your story as follows:

1. Your balance sheet

Your company's balance sheet provides a snapshot of what your company owns versus what it owes. It is the company scorecard and one of the quickest ways for an outside to tell if you're winning or losing the game. Comparing the year-over-year statistics gives an outside viewer a glimpse of how you're progressing at building a strong foundation of assets. This is one of the strongest arguments for building up retained earnings in your organization (depending on your corporate structure).

Some types of businesses (such as professional service businesses) have few if any tangible assets (meaning things that can be touched, tested and readily valued and sold). In that case, the balance sheet will often show a high number for goodwill or "blue sky". These were created in an attempt to quantify the value of intangible things like your business' reputation in the community, its brand recognition or the longevity of its client relationships. Founders who own such businesses need to pay special attention to how they document the value of their business, as few lenders will provide financing for primarily goodwill-based businesses.

2. Your income statement

If your balance sheet is the scorecard, the income statement is the play by play. Your income statement documents the earnings and expense history of your business. This is different from your cash flow statement described below. The income statement is where your revenues, expenses (including depreciation taken on your assets) are shown. Most importantly, the income statement shows your profit and loss.

Many business owners make it a habit to arrange their revenues and expenses such that their company either doesn't show a profit or otherwise keeps profits under certain levels in order to take advantage of lower tax brackets. This is a legitimate tax planning practice as long as it is done within the limits of the applicable laws. However, I offer a word caution on this practice because, while it may feel good to pay less tax year to year, your annual tax planning ought to be done in consideration of your long-term goals for the company. Basically, a business that hasn't shown a profit in the past 18 years may be a lot harder to sell, simply because you'll have to reverse a lot of accounting wizardry (hopefully legal wizardry) to prove to your buyer the company has been profitable.

Your buyer doesn't want to have to take a forensic accounting class just to understand your financial statements. Buyers are not impressed by how smart you believe you are for outmaneuvering the IRS or how much tax you have saved yourself over the years. Drawn out discussions about your historical formulas and strategies do not create confidence. They create suspicion. They send buyers a warning signal with regard to two things: A). Future audit risk and B). Complexity.

3. Your statement of cash flow

Remember when your crazy aunt got you a plastic box full of ants for your 8th birthday? Yes, I too once had an ant farm. I enjoyed watching those ants crawl around in their sand-filled prison for about 3 days before it just got too weird. I don't know if stores still sell those but I hope not. I'm sure some college student has started a non-profit organization by now arguing for the sanctity of ant lives.

The statement of cash flows for your business is a bit like the ant farms of old. It provides a spectator's view of how cash moves around through your business over short periods of time. The statements typically chart inflows and outflows on a month-to-month basis. The idea is to give you an understanding of your business' typical payment and expense cycles.

What is great about having a record of your statement of cash flows is you can establish long trend lines (there's that word again). Trend lines are the quickest way to evaluate whether you're moving forward or backward, sinking or soaring, drifting or... you get the idea.

I will say it again because it's worth repeating: Context, Context, and Context. As the chief storyteller of your business, having a history of cash flow statements helps communicate to your prospective buyer what to expect after purchasing your business. It helps them predict when they will start to see return on investment and what they should consider normal in terms of your cash payments and receipts.

4. Your tax returns

1040, Schedule C, K-1s, AMT, ABC, XYZ... it all starts sounding like alphabet soup after awhile. However, your tax returns are a vital tool for telling the story of your business. They serve a few useful functions besides calculating the Government's annual profit share though. Your tax returns are the ultimate "true-up" on your business' finances. They are the official, legal documents which trace everything you own from year to year, how it's accounted for, what came in, what went out, how much you paid everyone (including yourself), how generous or stingy you are with your benefits and multiple other data points.

Many tax professionals pride themselves on one thing: reducing tax. However, the best ones know that reducing or limiting tax is really only one part of the picture. It is just one strategy among many to help a business owner accomplish her or his goals. There are times when it can make sense to pay more tax. Blasphemy? Maybe not.

Depending on the type of business you have, consistent and growing retained earnings inside your business can be one of the key indicators of a healthy, well-capitalized business. A business that never holds cash and pays out everything it has at year end to its owner(s) bears a striking resemblance to your out of work nephew who spends whatever he gets, has no savings and is always stressed about making rent. Some business owners get into the habit of draining all earnings out of the business and then financing operations by making personal loans back to the corporation.

This may sound like a good investment on the surface and _can_ be a useful tax-planning tool in some instances. The company is paying you interest and creating a deductible expense for itself. Everybody wins, right? This can work in some situations but can create issues when you go to sell. It can be especially troublesome when the loans are not repaid in full and build up over time (for instance, when the business is running cash flow negative during lean periods).

Constantly loaning money back to your corporation can result in a business that has a large liability on the books that either must be repaid before the shares are sold (in a stock purchase arrangement) or must be forgiven by the lender (you). The first option is usually unattractive to the buyer and the second option leaves you without the cash you thought was coming back to you with interest and potential tax issues. Nobody wins.

I'm not saying every business should intentionally pay more tax than they otherwise have to. However, it is critical that you ask the various members of your success team to evaluate your tax planning in light of your overall goals. Building a business you can position for sale may call for a more balanced approach to tax management.

5. Your core metric dashboard

One of my mentors loves to remind me, "Whatever gets measured gets done.". Those are words to live by and I go back to them every time I don't feel I'm making progress in any area of life.

Your core metrics are the set of internal data points you have determined to be the most critical to your business success. For instance, most service businesses only have three options when they want to grow. First, they can acquire new clients to sell their services to. Second, they can try to persuade their existing clients to buy new stuff from them. Third, they can persuade their existing clients to buy the same stuff from them more often.

Given those options:

- How would an owner know which strategy would produce the fastest, most consistent results if she wanted to grow her revenue by 30% in the next 12 months?

- Would she know how many new people she has to contact before she could expect to record a new sale?

- Would she know how much more an existing customer buys from her on average after she conducts a "thank you" campaign?

- How about how often her top 10 clients purchase each of her products or services?

- It would be an intuitive guess at best if she weren't tracking the core metrics for the business.

Creating a detailed core metric dashboard allows you to further enhance the story of your business for a buyer. It's like creating a recipe book for your business' success. Once you have the recipe, you can show the buyer, "Look, we know what we do well, we know how we do it, we know why we do it that way and what our customers like. Follow this recipe and you'll be successful too.".

Finally, understand that your buyer is valuing your business based on their perception of its future moneymaking potential. It is a forward-looking perspective. You are valuing your business based on what it has already accomplished in the past. It is a rearview perspective. You can put your business in a very appealing light by having each of these pieces of your story up to date and arranged in a compelling order.

Remedy #2: Become the chief historian of your business. Make sure you're using all the tools available to tell its story in a way that helps your buyer see it the way you do.

Chapter 9: The Third Big Flub - Failing to Identify What Is Most Important Before Negotiations Start

My wife and I had an odd experience with this Flub when we moved into a new house a few years ago. The new place was exactly what we were looking for. It was in the neighborhood we wanted, in the best school district and near the church we attended. Best of all - it was close to our target price. To our dismay, negotiations stalled after a few volleys back and forth. Even more dismaying, we learned they had stalled over a lamp.

To be fair, it was a chandelier. The seller loved her decor and took great pride in each item. In her view, the final price of the home ought to reflect the quality of the fixtures she was leaving behind and she simply couldn't reconcile a price reduction on the entire house (the item we were most interested in) while it contained this particular chandelier she loved so much. She viewed the chandelier as the most important thing in that moment.

We really weren't concerned about the chandelier other than that it was attached to the ceiling in the house we really wanted. The final contract was written to have the chandelier replaced with a new ceiling fan. We moved into the house. The seller moved on with her life (and her lamp). Everyone walked away happy.

Could you imagine if the whole deal fell apart because neither of us was able to clarify what we were most interested in owning? The seller would have kept her chandelier but not sold the house she no longer wanted. We wouldn't have gotten the house we really wanted because it was attached to a chandelier we didn't care about. Similarly, when I hear people say they want to sell their business, I'm compelled to ask what they really intend to sell. In other words, what is most important to them?

Your business isn't just one thing. I mentioned in a previous chapter how your business is really a complex organism. You have client lists, trade secrets, stock certificates, sometimes multiple brand names, desks, computers, copy machines, refrigerators, staff people, staff procedures, rents, known debts, hidden liabilities, pension plans and funding vehicles... Are you selling all of that or just a few pieces? Which ones? Why those ones?

One of the best things you can do as you prepare to sell your business is to put down on paper the top three things you want to accomplish through the sale. These may be lifestyle goals, financial outcomes or to just shed liabilities. I have spent many hours in discovery meetings over the years having this exact conversation and it is surprising how few clients have clarity on this point and yet are absolutely convinced they need to take some specific course of action.

Another mentor of mine used to tell me how most people's goals generally fall into five Mores and one Less as follows:

More Money - This one seems fairly obvious but most people will continue to want more money no matter how much they already have. It takes a special person to say, "No, I have enough.". Our relationship with money is very complex and the roots of our desire for it go down deep into our emotions and our overall psyche. A constant desire for more money tends to stem from two places emotionally though. It either comes from a desire for more security or from a competitive drive in which money represents the scorecard. Most people I encounter do list "more money" somewhere near the top of their list of goals no matter what the reason is.

More Time - What's the purpose of having more money if you don't have the time to enjoy it? Business owners in particular know that it can take every spare second to keep the lights on. Between employee issues, new customer acquisition and putting out fires with existing issues there is sometimes little time leftover for family or friends. Few people arrive at the end of their life wishing they spent more time at work though. While long hours are usually necessary for a season of life to keep the business going, almost everyone reaches a point where they want to create time to just enjoy life.

More Meaning - Money is great but mature people eventually begin to desire something more. Being recognized for our achievements or finding meaning in life are also important motivators. These become more prominent especially as we get older. I haven't met the person yet whose motivating factors include dying alone in insignificant anonymity. The search for meaning and recognition that will live on as a legacy is common across cultures, socioeconomic status and even across time.

More Power - A desire for power really comes down to a desire for control. It may seem counter intuitive that people who own their companies or are in charge of organizations large or small could feel out of control. They don't have a boss and can set their own schedule. What more could they ask for? However, recognize that many businesses get started with a simple idea. That simple idea grows and the systems required to support the growth become more complex. A person who had a simple idea for a product or service can quickly find himself or herself at the helm of something that has grown beyond their original skill set.

Few people are simultaneously gifted as an engineer, a salesperson, a human resources director, an accountant, a headhunter, an operations engineer, a graphics designer, marketing specialist and a logistics manager. Yet all of these functions are required to run a successful business. You can see how a person could start to feel out of control quickly without the proper support systems and team in place as their company grows. The desire for power or control as it pertains to selling a business is about wanting to take back control of your life, your schedule and your destiny.

More (and Deeper) Relationship - Even the rich and powerful have a desire to feel connected to other people and to be loved. Perhaps your lifestyle goals are rooted in this desire and the strategies to reach them will focus on creating stronger relationships. This goal may also lead you to pursue new things and expand your network of relationships. People were created to live in community with others so it's not surprising that this goal is common across all levels of society.

Less Stress - Stress has become a way of life in American culture. The normal pressures of daily life become magnified when you are the one signing the checks each month. I don't know of anyone who enters retirement desiring more stress in their life so this one definitely makes the list of top lifestyle goals for most business owners.

The list above is not exhaustive but it will help get you started. I suggest having a meaningful conversation (or a series of meaningful conversations) with your husband, your wife or a trusted advisor to help you clarify your goals before you even begin the process of selling your business.

Many of the items outlined above can be achieved without having to sell a business at all. There are many instances in which a few changes to the company procedures or making a key hire can allow the owner to achieve his or her goals while still maintaining control of their business. The key question to ask is, "Do I really want out or do I just want things to be different?".

If you do determine that achieving your goals necessitates selling the business, the next step then becomes determining what specific assets (or combination of assets) to sell in order to achieve the outcomes you are seeking. This is yet another time when your success team will prove their value. There are two primary ways a business is sold. The first is by completing a stock sale in which the shares of the company are transferred to a new owner. The second is by selling the company's assets to the buyer.

There are advantages and drawbacks to each. It is critical that you discuss these options with your success team and assess what liabilities and opportunities you are accepting as a result of either of these options. Your buyer may assume your asking price includes things like accounts receivable or other revenue streams, which are related to but separate from the business.

An example of this would be a chiropractor that also is part of a multi-level marketing program selling dietary supplements through his practice. Those are technically two different businesses; customer lists, marketing systems and revenue streams. However, a buyer who sees the products on the shelves in the lobby could be lead to believe they are part of the deal if not clarified up front.

More disclosure in more detail is usually the safer course of action even if it seems overkill. Courts tend to look more favorably on the buyer in situations when fraud or misrepresentation is alleged. Winding up in a lawsuit is bound to take you off track as you pursue your five mores and your less.

Remedy #3: Be specific about your goals for the sale, what is most important and what specifically you intend to sell before the buyer shows up.

Chapter 10: The Fourth Big Flub - Failing to Execute

I got my undergraduate degree from Azusa Pacific University. There was a student who preceded me by several years whose name was revered by everyone in the School of Business and Management. His name was Zach Miller.

Some said Zach Miller signed his first real estate deal in crayon while having his diaper changed. Others regaled me with stories of how Zach was running three businesses off campus during his junior year. Still others swore Zach was worth more than the Dean by the time he graduated. It also seemed like there wasn't a freshman in my class who didn't claim to have some kind of connection to Zach on his next business deal (though nothing ever seemed to materialize).

I saw Zach at an event on campus in the spring of my sophomore year. I sat breathlessly in the auditorium that day waiting to see the man I had heard so much about. I hoped to glean some morsel of insight that would help me make my first million before I had my degree.

Suddenly, the lights went down and the cheers went up. There he was. He wore an expensive blue suit, no tie and his hair was combed in the messy "I'm-so-cool-

I-just-got-out-of-bed-and-walked-up-here" look that was popular at the time. His speech lasted all of about 3 minutes. Here's what he said:

"Do you know what separates me from all of you? There's only one reason why I'm up here and you're all sitting out there. It's because I execute. While you sit there planning how you're going to start a business and make a ton of money, I'm actually starting businesses and making a ton of money. You look at a piece of real estate and think how cool it would be if you could buy it. I actually go buy it. You plan, you think, you hesitate. I do. That's why I'm up here and you're out there. If you want to make money, you have to execute. Forget planning. Just execute. Otherwise, you'll never be up here with me." With that said, he walked off the stage.

At first I thought he was just being arrogant. The more I thought about it though, the more I realized he was absolutely right. You can have the best plan in the world but never achieve your goals if you don't cross the line and execute it. This principle is critical in selling a business.

Taking action can be difficult because it involves moving forward in spite of the unknown. We all have our hang-ups, fears and attachments which prevent us from taking action. Fear leads to rationalization, which perpetuates inaction.

Fear is natural. It keeps us alive. Fear can also be a major obstacle to execution though. Fears can be rational like the fear felt by a surfer as he sees a sixteen foot gray shadow swim underneath him while he's waiting for the next waves to roll in. Fear can also be completely irrational like my fear I would be bitten by a shark in our family swimming pool as a kid. True fact: I wouldn't go in our pool at night until I was in high school. I blame Steven Spielberg.

These delusions affect us all everyday to various degrees. They are fear-generated stories we believe to justify why we should or shouldn't do something. The fact that they are obviously not true doesn't make these delusions any less powerful. There are four delusions I encounter frequently with business owners that keep them from taking action on their succession plan. I have named them The Snow White, The James Bond, The Tigger and The Suffering Savior.

Delusion #1 - The Snow White - Someday my prince will come!

Anyone with daughters should be familiar with this scenario. A damsel in distress. Talking forest creatures that befriend her. A rider on a white horse slays the dragon. A hastily executed teen wedding and a happily ever after.

The Snow White delusion usually appears when people are focused on the Sale door. The problem is they haven't done the groundwork necessary to make their business sale-able, their staff and operations systems aren't ready for a transition to an outside buyer and they haven't done their valuation to know what the business is actually worth. Despite all of this, they still believe deep down that someone will eventually show up at their door and offer to write them a check for the exact amount they think they need for their retirement. They believe they will take the check, hand over the keys and ride off into the sunset with millions of dollars in their wallet and no more problems.

It seems silly when you read it in print. However, this scenario (or one like it) is the number one delusion that keeps business owners from executing a well-crafted plan to sell their business. Why plan when your white knight is just beyond the edge of the forest?

Delusion #2 - The James Bond - Everyone is a double agent.

You will recognize this right away if you've seen any of the films in James Bond franchise. Bond is sitting in a crowded hotel bar when he is approached by a stranger. The stranger pulls out a ridiculously feeble weapon to execute a surprise attack. Agent 007 quickly disarms him. Suddenly, the entire wait staff reveals they are part of the gang of thugs hired by the villain. After they've all been dispatched, the bar tender pulls out a bazooka from below the bar and Bond leaps from the window to the street below just as the bar explodes. He coolly gets into a waiting car on the street, kisses a buxom blonde woman and speeds away from the scene.

The James Bond delusion also appears most often with the Sale door option but can also be present for Succession-focused sellers. The owner says he wants to sell. However, when interested parties inquire, he acts like it's a double agent coming to get them. They start looking for all the reasons the buyer is the wrong person to transition to. Suspicion runs wild and the founder often ends up being the saboteur of his own success. It comes down to a lack of trust and lack of confidence in his preparations.

What the James Bond is really saying is "I don't want to engage with this person because I'm afraid of what they might say or do. What if they don't like my business? What if they don't think it's worth the asking price? What if they're conspiring with someone else to try and get a lower price? Attack!".

Don't let James Bond be in the driver's seat. Set your asking price based on a realistic, data-driven valuation. Hire a qualified attorney to draft your non-disclosure documents. Insist on having everything in writing. Work with a qualified team coordinating for you success. Trust and verify. Then move forward.

Delusion #3 - The Tigger - I'm the only one!

Do you know what the most wonderful thing about a Tigger is according to Tigger? He's the only one! You never know what to expect from him. There's no playbook or rules to follow. He's not accountable to anyone because no one really can say whether his behavior is normal based on a wide survey of the local Tigger population. Best of all, whatever Tigger is doing is what he does best!

This is how some business owners see themselves. The Tigger stripes show up at the first mention that someone else could be a potential successor for them. The emotions can really get ramped up especially when the successor is a generation younger than the founder. They feel no one could take as good of care of their clients as they do. No one else could sell as much as they do. No one else could deal with all the daily problems and menial tasks as effectively as they do. No one else can do everything exactly the way they do it. What could some young punk possibly bring to the table that he or she hasn't already thought of? "No! I'm the only one!"

First of all, if a business owner is doing everything in their business, I can almost guarantee they're not doing anything with excellence. That's going to trickle down to unsatisfied customers, which will mean they buy less and the business earns less. It also means fewer referrals, which means lower long-term growth. The Tigger's organization chart often looks like this:

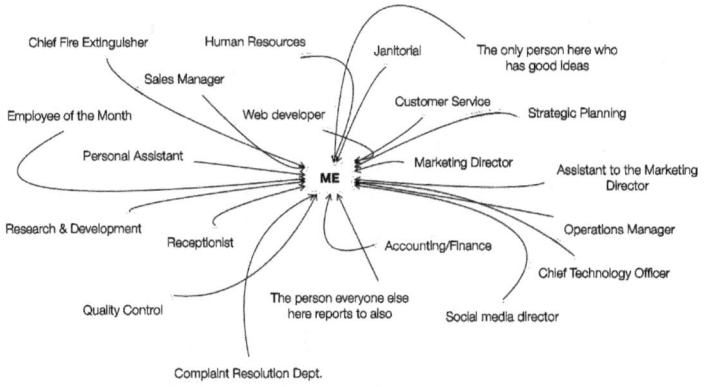

That business is actually going to be more difficult to sell but not because it inherently lacks value. It's because the business owner doesn't trust their people enough to allow them to apply their gifts, talents and skills to their jobs. The owner creates more work for him or herself and actually makes the business less valuable. Instead, their transition needs to first emphasize building systems and an environment where employees are free to do their jobs, are held accountable and make the business more valuable by their efforts.

Delusion #4 - The Suffering Savior - So others may live.

I once had a business owner tell me, "I'll probably just die here at my desk. They'll come find me keeled over here one morning. But at least I'll go out doing what I love.". I stared back at him blankly.

That guy had spent the last hour telling me how stressed out he was, how badly he wanted to retire and how he was having major health issues as a result of being a workaholic. He was miserable. Yet that was his response when I asked him what he thought about creating a transition plan so he could retire in 12 months. He didn't know if or how his business could survive without him. His plan was to die instead.

The Suffering Savior believes he or she is somehow special or their business is different than every other business. They play the martyr and decide it is nobler to go down with the ship rather than do the work required to make a successful transition happen. Everyone else seems to have so much luck but not them. They have suffered for years creating jobs for others while they themselves will never be able to retire.

I think it's because people tend to wrap a moral or spiritual calling around this delusion that it seems to be the hardest to break free from. If this sounds familiar to you or reminds you of someone you know, shake her up! News flash: The Savior already came and you aren't him!

The key to breaking free from the Suffering Savior delusion is to develop a new vision for what life could be like after the transition and start taking small steps in that direction. The founder needs to recognize they aren't the only one who wants to do a great job for his or her customers. Next, they need to focus on a clear and compelling reason why it's worth it to take action.

What does he want MORE than what he has now? WHY does he want that? What is MOST important?

The Four Delusions are the repeat offenders keeping so many business owners from executing. Instead of giving in to these false beliefs, make a decision to take action. If you find yourself coming up with reasons you can't spare one hour to address this stuff, pull the monster out of the closet, give it a name and send it packing. You have to execute.

Remedy #4: Execute. Do it every day. Do it right now.

Chapter 11: The Fifth Big Flub - Failing to Invest In A Success Team

Let me tell the story of two very different millionaires: John Carpenter and Isaac Caldiero. John Carpenter was an IRS employee who became the first contestant in history to win one million dollars on ABC's *Who Wants to Be a Millionaire?* game show on November 19, 1999. He didn't use a single lifeline[7] and only stumbled briefly on one question during his march to a million bucks. He later went on to win an additional $125,000 on a subsequent episode featuring previous winners.

Isaac Caldiero used to wait tables in a restaurant before becoming the first winner of $1,000,000 on NBC's *American Ninja Warrior* competition. If you're not familiar with the show, contestants have to make their way through an extreme obstacle course that tests agility, balance, grip strength, jump height and overall endurance. Don't think balance beams and ball pits. Think hyper-caffeinated chimpanzees swinging through the jungle canopy at full speed.

Isaac is acknowledged to be one of the best rock climbers in the world. Prior to competing on the show, he lived in his van and had never made more

---

[7] Carpenter actually used one lifeline to call his father before he answered the final question. He called just to say he knew the answer and he was about to win $1,000,000.

than \$10,000 in a year. His final challenge was to complete a four-stage obstacle course that included an eight story, 75-foot vertical rope climb in less than 30 seconds. His entire life had been a preparation for that course and he conquered it.

Unlike John Carpenter who had all the answers by himself, Isaac had spent almost a decade training with a close-knit group of climbers and obstacle course junkies. He and his training partners called themselves The Wolf Pack and his buddies were all there cheering him on until the very last second. Both men ended up with the million bucks (well... about \$600,000 after taxes) but they took very different approaches.

Selling a business (heck, just running a business) is more like competing on *American Ninja Warrior* than *Who Wants To Be A Millionaire.* Unless your name is John Carpenter, you probably should not try and go it alone. Most people will find they can achieve greater things in life when they are surrounded by a group of trusted advisors helping them avoid pitfalls, stay on course and move forward when they feel like quitting. I call it a Success Team because that's the purpose of hiring them. The goal is to assemble a team of excellent advisors across different disciplines all dedicated to working together for your success.

One of the things I inquire about during a discovery meeting with a new client is whom they seek advice from in the different areas of their life. We examine where they go for financial advice, business advice, relationship advice, spiritual advice, etc. Besides each person's name, I ask four follow up questions:

1). How did you meet him or her?

2). What is your relationship like?

3). Is he or she doing a good job for you?

4). How do you know?

The responses range from simple shrugs of "I don't know" to "Yeah, they do a good job I guess.". Very rarely do I encounter someone who can answer the last question with confidence either to the positive or negative. It doesn't surprise me when I hear it from people who are broke. It's shocking to hear it from people worth millions of dollars.

Achieving your life's most important goals is something you simply cannot do by yourself. You must have a solid team in place to support you and each member on the team should be committed to two things 1). Applying their full skills, resources and knowledge to your situation and 2). Collaborating with other professionals on the team.

Both of the criteria above are important and not always easy to find. Some professionals are competent but stretched too thin to focus their resources enough to produce excellent results. They are usually generalists who will take anyone who walks through their door as a client.

The second issue is ego. I've run into so many professionals who consider it their job to be the filter and final word on any advice given to the client. They are unyielding, self-interested and more concerned about receiving all the credit than producing the results the client needs. They stifle the planning process and limit the free flow of ideas. You can find these people in any profession - tax, legal, insurance, financial advice, business coaching - and they're toxic. They're takers instead of givers and you do not want them on your team.

The makeup of your success team should reflect your business and your life circumstances. Everyone on the team is going to get paid at some point so you should also consider aligning their compensation style and timing with your needs and budget.

Here are the core team members you should start with:

Tax Professional - I suggest you start by recruiting your tax pro for three reasons. First, they are typically the most flexible/scalable in tailoring their services or advice to your needs and budget. Second, they often have experience across a wide range of businesses and you're more likely to find one who has worked with companies like yours before. Third, tax planning is relevant and urgent no matter what you do in business or what stage of the business lifecycle you're at.

Your tax professional could be a Certified Public Accountant (CPA), an Enrolled Agent (EA) or a Tax Attorney. The IRS Manual sets out specific rules for which professionals may represent a taxpayer before the IRS and who may prepare taxes for others. You can find the publication on the IRS website by going to:

http://www.irs.gov/irm/part1/irm_01-025-001.html

Each of these designations comes with varying levels of training and education. The requirements for becoming a CPA vary from state to state but most require 150 semester-hours of instruction. That's 30 hours more than most bachelor's degrees. In addition, some states will require a minimum number of semester hours of accounting-specific instruction, and a minimum number of hours of business instruction. They also must pass a four-part exam.

In contrast, becoming an enrolled agent can be done by completing a short educational course, obtaining a pin number from the IRS, passing a standardized government test and making sure your own taxes are up to date. Both can file your tax returns but there can be a big difference in experience and educational background.

This isn't to say there aren't some highly qualified EAs out there and some dismally poor CPAs in practice. It just should be a reminder to understand the differences, ask the right questions, get reference checks and make sure the person filling this spot in your success team has the qualifications you need to reach your goals.

Financial Planner - Once you have your tax professional seat filled, the next person I recommend you identify would be your Financial Planner. This term has become muddled over the years but financial planning is really a process rather than a single service. Their are six stages to the process as defined by the Certified Financial Planner Board of Standards as follows:

1). Establishing and defining the relationship between the client and the advisor.

2). Gathering the necessary client data to asses the current situation.

3). Analyzing the data.

4). Developing and presenting the financial planning recommendations

5). Implementing the plan

6). Monitoring the plan and making changes as necessary

You can see how this process could be used to address a wide range of issues for a client. That's partially why there has been so much confusion as to what a Financial Planner really does. The process can include investment advice, insurance analysis, estate planning, education planning, business counsel, retirement advice, charitable gift planning and wide range of other issues. It all depends on what the client wants to achieve and what the adviser's specialty is. The process for helping a client achieve the goals remains the same though.

The key to remember here is a real Financial Planner's focus is on the development and implementation of a sound plan that has a high statistical probability of achieving the client's objectives within the timeframe desired. The planning itself is the focus and purpose of hiring her or him.

This is as opposed to what many companies in the insurance and investment industry have done which is use the term *financial plan* as a buzzword to lure prospects in. Once they're in the office, the financial plan the client thought they were getting is really nothing more than an elaborate sales tool to induce them to buy whatever insurance, annuity or investment product is being pitched that month. It's a bait and switch.

The key word to remember when hiring a Financial Planner for your team is FIDUCIARY (say it with me: fi-doo-she-air-ee). Being a fiduciary means your Financial Planner has a legal obligation to make recommendations that are solely in your best interest as his or her client. They also have a legal obligation to disclose any potential conflicts of interest. This is as opposed to someone who may call him or herself a financial planner but is actually an insurance salesperson, annuity salesperson, mutual fund salesperson or a stockbroker.

Advisers in the latter categories are only held to a standard of suitability. A non-fiduciary adviser generally has no legal obligation to disclose or avoid conflicts of interest in giving advice. It also means they can pretty much recommend anything they're licensed to sell so long as those recommendations could be deemed "suitable" by a prudent person who had the same limited information.

The vagueness of the suitability standard makes it difficult to hold an adviser accountable for providing bad advice. There's also no way to really be confident the recommendations you're receiving on a particular product or strategy are being given because that's the best thing for you. It could just as easily be because that's the product the adviser's home office gets the highest bonus on this month. As long as an argument could be made in court that anybody with the same information could have reasonably made a similar recommendation, the client is usually going to be stuck and the adviser can walk away without repercussions. It may seem subtle but the difference can be huge in terms of the quality of advice you receive.

To help you identify a proper Financial Planner, look for the CFP® marks. Achieving the CERTIFIED FINANCIAL PLANNER™ Professional designation requires completion of the Four E's

Education: A bachelor's degree is required to obtain the designation. In addition, potential certificants must complete a college-level course of study that takes an average of two years.

Examination: After a person has successfully met the education coursework requirement, they become eligible to register for the CFP® Certification Examination. The CFP® Certification Examination assesses the person's ability to apply their financial planning knowledge, in an integrated format, to financial planning situations. The test requires potential certificants to demonstrate expert-level knowledge across 84 planning related topics. It is administered over 10 hours spread across two days.

Experience - The CFP Board requires certificants to have three years of professional experience in the financial planning process, or two years of apprenticeship experience that meets additional requirements.

Ethics - CFP® professionals agree to adhere to the high standards of ethics and practice outlined in CFP Board's *Standards of Professional Conduct* and to acknowledge CFP Board's right to enforce them through its *Disciplinary Rules and Procedures*. After completing the education, examination and experience components of the CFP® certification, the advisor must complete a final application on which they are asked to disclose information about their background, including their involvement in any criminal, civil, governmental, or self-regulatory agency proceeding or inquiry, bankruptcy, customer complaint, filing, termination/internal reviews conducted by their employer or firm. CFP Board conducts a detailed background check for all candidates, including review of any disclosures made on the CFP® Certification Application. The CFP Board's Standards of Conduct can be downloaded directly from their website at <u>CFP.net</u>.

There is a big difference between the licensing requirements to become a financial advisor or an insurance agent and the certification requirements to obtain and keep the CERTIFIED FINANCIAL PLANNER™ Professional certification. I suggest anyone looking to hire a financial planner for the success team requires him or her to be a fiduciary and a CFP®!

Business & Estate Planning Attorneys - Imagine you're at your pediatrician's office. As he finishes up examining your kid's sore throat, you start telling him how concerned you are about your father's upcoming open-heart surgery. He perks up with interest saying, "Oh I do that too. Why don't you talk to my receptionist on the way out and we can just get him scheduled here next week?".

You pause, wondering if you heard that correctly. You ask "I thought you were a Pediatrician. Are you saying you're also a heart surgeon?".

He responds, "Oh, well my specialty is pediatrics but we all take the same classes in medical school. I can do heart surgery too if that's what you need. Just check with my receptionist and we can get your dad scheduled here next week.".

How likely would you been to take him up on his offer? If it were me, I'd take my kid and run!

Obviously, no one is going to allow their Pediatrician to handle their father's open-heart surgery. Yet they don't think they ought to have a specialist addressing their diverse legal needs. Many people assume that their estate planning attorney can handle all of their business legal needs, their business attorney can handle their estate planning, their family law attorney can also file their trademark applications, etc. They're all lawyers, right? What's the big deal?

The legal profession is as diverse as the medical profession. There are nuances to each field and the laws themselves are always changing in response to new legislation or new interpretations of old legislation. For the sake of convenience, you could identify a firm offering multiple specialty services by different attorneys. However, I typically suggest filling the estate planning attorney seat and the business attorney seat with different specialists.

Insurance Professionals - Life is full of risk. For every risk, there's a smiling insurance salesman willing to sell you a policy to cover it. Life insurance, long-term care insurance, disability, property casualty insurance, and professional liability insurance - each of these coverages may be necessary at different stages of your life. You may need to interview different specialists or have a few "on call" insurance professionals for when a new need is identified.

Once again, the same principle applies as in the legal field. Insurance is about managing specific types of risk. A great insurance professional will take the time to understand the specific risks you are faced with and identify several potential strategies to make sure you are protected. They should also be ready to bring in a specialist if their expertise doesn't match your need. Just because they're licensed to sell a certain type of policy doesn't mean they're the expert to handle the risk management in that area.

Personal Banker - In the old days, being a banker meant something more than working at the front counter in the bank. Your banker was a person who was familiar with your family and your business and partnered with you to match the bank's products to meet your capital financing needs. The focus was on personal service and the relationships were long term. I can tell you the old days still exist. You just have to know where to look.

The personal banker seat on your success team may be one of the most critical to getting your business transition completed. I suggest interviewing your personal banker with the same rigorous process you would use to interview a new employee. Identify several candidates and be sure to let them know you are also interviewing other options.

Don't just accept the recent college grad they try and give you when you first walk in. Spend time talking with the branch manager first. Discuss what you're looking for and ask about their approach to evaluating client needs. You will want to find out whom their portfolio of products are designed for (their ideal customer). Ask how long each of their bankers has been in the business.

Your goal is to identify someone who has a long track record in the banking business (preferably with the same bank) and has experience working with businesses with capital needs similar to yours. Be certain your chosen bank has the ability to provide the financing for the kind of transition you are considering. For instance, some lenders will not finance purchases of goodwill-based businesses. Your transition may call for your successor to obtain outside financing for the purchase so you are not reliant on Junior for your monthly paycheck once you're out of the business. Make sure your banker won't bail on you right before you're ready to make the transition.

You could also ask the other professionals on your team whether they have any recommendations for a personal banker who could fit your needs. Different banks focus on particular industries and specialties ranging from construction to agriculture or international trade. Your tax professional and your Financial Planner in particular should have a strong network of professionals whom they have vetted. As a final word on this, you will most likely have a more personalized experience when working with smaller, regional banks or specialty banks rather than one of the larger, national or even multi-national banks.

Business & Strategic Coach – There are only two ways to gain experience in business. The first requires time and the second requires money. Founders typically gained their business acumen over years of trial and error that honed their current business strategy. Their revenue and personal income grew incrementally each time they successfully adapted to the demands of the market. Neither the value of the business nor the high personal income associated with owning that business appeared overnight. In contrast, successors usually enter the business far down stream from those early touch-and-go days where the future success and viability of the business were still uncertain.

Handing off a successful, going business to an untested successor is like a fireman asking a bystander to hold the fire hose at full force. The water may continue to flow, but there's no telling how many bystanders are going to get soaked before the fire is out. This brings us to the second option for gaining experience: Engaging a business & strategic coach.

The term "succession" in itself should give you a clue as to how to proceed. Succession indicates a transfer of success from one to another. Hiring a business and strategic coach to come alongside your successor allows them to both take responsibility for the operation of the business (i.e. not have to keep coming back to you for advice) and also creates a support structure so they can borrow expertise while gaining his or her own business experience.

I definitely suggest engaging a strategic coach prior to completing the transition to the next generation in a succession strategy. An experienced strategic coach will act as a bridge of experience between the generations. It can also alleviate the tension from a founder not wanting to have too many things changed at once and the successor wanting to do it all his or her way. Both generations need to buy into the new strategy to create continuity.

Family Coach - What do the Disney family, Pritzker family (one time owners of the Hyatt Hotels brand) and the Dow Jones Family have in common? Besides being among the top wealthiest families in the country at one time or another, all have had their family wealth radically reduced and scattered as a result of family infighting. The latter two actually sold all or major portions of the companies that were the original source of the family wealth as part of the final settlements.

Research conducted by The Williams Group, Russ Alan Prince and other advisors and researchers of the wealthiest families around the world confirms less than 30% of families will successfully transfer their wealth to the second generation. Fewer than 10% will make it to the third. There's a truism in the legacy planning industry that says, "Shirtsleeves to shirtsleeves within three generations". It's been that way for decades and the reason may surprise you. It is not for lack of counsel. In the example of the families above, each one had access to the most sophisticated legal, financial and tax advice money could buy.

In each example, the #1 factor negatively impacting their wealth was a breakdown of trust and communication within the family. It makes sense if you think about it. What high school teacher shows kids how to respectfully disagree with their high-achieving parents on issues pertaining to the business they've been running for the past 30 years? Which class in college teaches how to be an active listener? Which class teaches humility and healthy family dynamics? None of them.

The role of the family coach is to help address the business of being a family rather than just the issues of running the family business. Most other professionals are not trained in the coaching skills needed to handle the role effectively, which is why I strongly suggest only engaging a trained family coaching organization for this role.

More information and resources for your family can be found as follows:

- The Williams Group website: **www.thewilliamsgroup.org**
- The Heritage Institute: **www.theheritageinstitute.com**
- Prince & Associates: **www.russalanprince.com**

Once you have your core team recruited, they can assist you in identifying which auxiliary professionals you ought to consider bringing in. Additional team members may include a business broker, venture capital partners, escrow officer, a commercial real estate broker, public relations experts, marriage & family therapist (no that's not a joke) or a family office executive. Rely on your core team members to identify and interview these auxiliary professionals. They tend to operate within close-knit networks and you might not be familiar with their particular niche.

Remedy #5: Invest time building a team of high performing expert advisers committed to working together for your success and the success of the next generation.

Chapter 12: Building Your Success Team

Now you know how critical it is to build a success team, I decided it would be cruel to leave you hanging. I've created an overview of how to prepare to interview them. It can feel uncomfortable sitting there in the office not knowing what to say because, let's face it; sometimes you don't know what you don't know. There are three things you ought to do when preparing for these interviews. Follow this guide and you will have your team assembled in no time.

Step 1: Pre-Interview Preparations

The first thing you need to do in preparing for your interview is write up the list of needs you want this person to fill. For example, you don't need to know everything a property casualty insurance agent does but you do know what your concerns are when it comes to being sued. You're going to write up a job description for each post based on what your concerns are in each area.

This can be as basic or elaborate as you like. Here is an example of a basic job description for your CPA:

- More than five years experience in practice

- Can give specific examples of experience she or he has had in working with businesses in my industry

- Firm is service focused and can provide specific examples of over-the-top service

- Has a guaranteed call-back time of not more than 24 hours

- More than one CPA working in the firm

- Takes a collaborative approach and regularly engages with their clients' other professionals

- Proactive planning focused rather than reactive or just the numbers

- Long tenured client base and can demonstrate how they've helped clients grow their business

- Has extensive network of other professionals they can introduce me to for the other seats on my success team

- Charges by project instead of hourly

It can be as simple as that. Think about the financial or business concerns that keep you awake at night. Write them down so you can discuss them with the person you're interviewing. You will want to build a list of at least three potential candidates for each seat on your team.

The place to start for building your list would be by asking whomever you already are working with. If you have a tax professional, ask them to provide names of three individuals they have worked with on a regular basis for the other seats on the team. They may not be able to come up with three for each but they can help you get started with at least a few. A caveat here would be to only ask your existing professional if you like working with them and plan to continue that relationship. You are not likely to get the right (or any) introductions from someone who knows you want to fire them.

The next place to look for candidates would be by reaching out to individuals whom you respect within any professional organizations, industry groups or business networking organizations such as your local Chamber of Commerce. I recommend only asking people who you view as more successful than you or whose success you would like to emulate. If you want what they have, you should do what they do and that includes getting access to their team.

Finally, if both of these first resources fail to provide enough names, you can search professional directories such as those contained in The Business Journal or by checking the following industry websites:

Financial Planners: www.cfp.net - they have a *Find A CFP® Professional* tool that is very useful.

Tax Professional: The National Directory of Certified Public Accountants provides list of qualified CPAs and some basic information about their specialties. You can search the database by visiting www.cpadirectory.com

Estate Attorney: The American College of Trusts and Estates Counsel has a list of potential candidates at www.actec.org.

Business Attorney: A list of potential business attorney candidates can be searched by visiting your State Bar Association website. They have tools to search for a lawyer by specialty and certification. For example, the Texas State Bar Association website can be found at www.texasbar.com. California's website is www.calbar.ca.gov. A Google search for "Your State" plus "Bar Association" will bring up your local one.

Insurance Professional: I suggest relying on your existing professional relationships for a referral to an insurance professional. Focus on finding the team members above first prior to wading into this one. Insurance professionals vary widely in their approach and you want to be sure whomever you choose is well vetted by other advisors prior to engaging them. Insurance can be one of the more controversial products and any purchases should be made after careful review with the whole team. True professionals are becoming harder to find in the insurance field and the best ones will have spent time developing relationships with professionals across industries so stick with who your other team members already know rather than going the directory route.

Personal Banker: Your CPA and your Financial Planner are going to be your best source of introductions for this seat. Nearly every bank has a person with the job title of Personal Banker. You are looking for the one in a thousand who are true professionals in the field.

Business & Strategic Coach: I suggest looking to one of the other members of your success team for an introduction to a business & strategic coach. You want to find someone who has demonstrated success in his or her own business endeavors and who specializes in your business _model_. Notice I did not say "specializes in your industry". The specifics of every business may be different even within the same industry. However, there are certain nuances of each business model that are repeatable no matter what industry they serve. Some examples of business model specialties are:

- Helping single location businesses launch new franchises

- Helping manufacturing businesses expand through supply chain management

- Helping domestic businesses sell internationally

- Helping traditional retailers expand into e-commerce

Your CPA, banker and financial planner should be good sources for introductions to credible business & strategic coaches. If that fails to turn up results, try checking the International Coach Federation website (www.coachfederation.org). I never recommend hiring a professional without proper vetting even if they carry impressive credentials behind their name. Use online searches and the ICF site as a starting point only. Once you identify a few potential coaches, proceed with the interview process accordingly. Make sure you get plenty of references to verify their results before moving forward. Coaching is about one thing – results. If they can't provide a strong track record of getting verifiable results for their clients, move on.

Family Coach: The family coaching field is still in its early stages of growth. There are groups who focus on different levels of family wealth so it's important to find someone who is matched to your family's current needs and resources. The Heritage Institute (www.theheritageinstitute.com) has an extensive network of trained family coaches and can help find someone local to you if the other members of your success team are unable to provide an introduction. The Family Office Exchange (www.familyoffice.com) can also be a valuable resource in finding a coach.

Step 2: The Interview Guide

Once you have identified candidates in each unfilled seat, it's time to schedule some interviews. I suggest doing the initial interview at their office instead of your office or home. This is potentially going to be a long-term partnership. You want to meet their other staff, make sure you feel comfortable in their office and that they present themselves as the high-caliber professional you need. In addition to bringing the list of needs you identified for each area above, here are the minimum questions I suggest you get answers to:

- Please describe your ideal client

- What are the three most important issues your clients are asking you about today and how are you addressing them?

- What percentage of your time is spent acquiring new clients verses serving existing clients?

- How many client-facing professionals (i.e. advice givers) are in the firm?

- Please tell me about your approach to serving clients.

- I'm interviewing several possible professionals. What differentiates you from your competitors?

- Can you describe how you get paid and your thoughts on how advisors ought to be compensated in your field?

- Do you have any revenue sharing agreements or pay/receive referral fees from other entities or professionals you do business with?

- Can you describe your continuation plan? In other words, what happens if you're no longer here one day?

- Do you have any plans to sell your practice in the next five years?

- Tell me about your approach to collaborating with outside professionals.

- Whom would I be working most if I were to engage your firm? Would I be working with you or an associate? How long have they been in practice/a part of your practice? (Same questions as above for him or her if you'll be working with someone else).

- If you were interviewing someone for this seat on the advisory team, what other questions would you be asking?

Lastly, you will want to also ask for introductions to other candidates for the different seats on your success team. In other words, you would ask for names of possible financial planners, insurance professionals or attorneys if you were interviewing a CPA.

You do not need to go into great detail about your plans for your company or your personal family wealth at this stage. There will be a time for that in a follow up interview once you have narrowed your list down to your top candidate. The goal of the interview session is to find out about THEM rather than to give them a chance to tailor their answers to your situation. You can close the interview by thanking them for their time, letting them know you have a few more interviews to conduct and that you will be reviewing the information with the other members of your success team before making any decisions.

The initial interview should be no more than one hour long. You want to respect their time but I wouldn't consider hiring a professional for my team who wasn't willing to invest 30 - 60 minutes with me up front to determine if they're the right fit for my needs.

Step 3: Hiring The Team

You've done your interviews and found the right candidates and now its time to execute. You will want to go back to each candidate and schedule a follow up meeting. It's during this time you can go into more detail about your circumstances and specifically what projects you anticipate having them help you on.

Before finalizing any agreement, each new professional should provide an engagement letter which outlines the scope of the services they will provide, sets expectations for timelines and roles as well as how they will be compensated. You can then ask your lead advisor (whomever you feel you have the closest relationship with) to reach out to schedule an introductory meeting so each member of the team can begin collaborating on your plan.

If you haven't figured it out by now, I am a big believer in seeking counsel from a number of trusted advisers before making important decisions. The members of your success team each bring unique expertise and they are an extremely valuable source of wisdom as your pursue your goals. I have invested time developing my own client advisory board to assist me in creating transition and wealth management plans for my clients. They have the option of adopting my advisory board as their success team if they choose to. They're free to work with their own team but having access to this turnkey option is an added value for the families who hire me.

I conducted interviews with several members of my client advisory board and I've included the transcripts of those interviews in the chapters that follow. Each interview provides great insight on different aspects of the succession planning process. My hope is to give you a small taste of what it's like when you're working with an experienced team to guide your planning. Now, let's move on to the third and final part of this book: The Client Advisory Board Member Interviews.

Part III: The Client Advisory Board Member Interviews

Disclaimer: The thoughts and opinions expressed in the following interviews are those of the respective interviewees exclusively. They do not necessarily represent the views of Adam Broughton, CFP®. Nothing contained herein is intended as specific tax or legal advice. Always seek counsel from qualified tax, legal and/or financial professionals before taking any action that could impact your business or personal finances.

Chapter 13: Michael J. Sackett – Sackett Financial Group

Michael Sackett is the founder of Sackett Financial Group in Brea, CA. He has been an entrepreneur, accountant, tax, financial and business advisor since 1980. His primary goal since then has been to help clients implement disciplines to achieve a level of financial independence that allows them to enjoy a comfortable and fulfilling lifestyle. His specialties include: business strategy, management reporting, tax planning, financial analysis, and problem resolution.

The following conversation took place on January 5, 2016 between Michael J. Sackett (Mike) and Adam Broughton, CFP®.

Here's What We Talk About:

- Should your CPA be talking about more than just your taxes?

- What are the key indicators a business is ready for a transition?

- Who belongs in which seats on the success team?

- Who should a client expect to lead the conversations with the success team?

- What questions should a founder be thinking about before choosing a successor?

- What are the major lifecycle phases of a founder should expect in his or her business and what are some best practices in each phase?

- What happens if you and your business partner(s) go your separate ways?

- Plus a whole lot more so read on!

Adam: Would you mind sharing with our readers a bit about yourself and about your professional background, Mike?

Mike: Sure. I started my accounting and tax practice back in 1980. Through the years, the businesses I worked with morphed a lot as time and technologies have changed. One of the biggest changes has been the adoption of computers versus when I first started when virtually nobody had them.

At the time I started, accounting people did accounting and tax. That was it. The idea of doing estate planning or wealth management or insurance was an abomination to the historical norms of the accounting profession. And so I stayed within those norms until the year 2000 in which that mentality became "old school". I got licensed in the securities arena, also in insurance, and started offering a more full scope of services to our clients. Again, when we first started, the idea of somebody in the accounting field handling multiple disciplines was blasphemy. Doing public-style accounting meant you would be independent of the organization or the ownership so that your work was a pristine independent statement as to a business' or taxpayer's true financial concern.

The maintenance of high standards is obviously essential but the role of the CPA has changed over time. The idea that you're entirely independent has largely gone away in the realm in which we practice. We changed from being a judge and jury about the financial condition of a business to being the great advocate for the entrepreneurial people that we work with. Our role now is to help them grow their net worth, both through running better businesses and through the accumulation of assets to be used post career after they've exited their business.

That's kind of a big change that many people in the accounting profession still don't want to accept. About 25% of us in the public accounting arena now offer this full spectrum of services. It's been a significant change over the last 35 years from what business was like then versus what it is now.

Adam: It sounds like transitioning from being in a data entry number crunching role to more of an advisory role has been where you've been moving.

Mike: Oh sure. Early in the profession you weren't even considered an advisor as a CPA. You were considered to be very independent of them and your job was to report to banks and creditors and investors the true operational activities of somebody's business or their personal tax scenario for the purposes of getting credit or reporting to investors. Now, it's so much different than that. You tend to be all in for the entrepreneur. You're really trying to wear two hats. You're trying to keep them compliant and honest, but you're also completely in on their side, trying to help them accumulate wealth.

Adam: What are the other seats at the table that need to be filled in terms of an advisory council if a business owner is going to have life-long success?

Mike: Well, I think the wealth advisory is essential as well as good legal counsel. Preferably, you've got a well-coordinated team between the wealth side, the tax side, and estate side of your financial spectrum. I think that the reason I say "well-coordinated" is people need to be on the same page.

As I've seen in my life, those things often don't all reconcile. We see estate plans that are in conflict with beneficiary designations on the life insurance policies or retirement plans or annuities. And that just comes flat out from lack of coordination and whether that be the fault of the advisors or the fault of the client, at the end of the day, it's always the client that gets hurt when those things happen.

It's always been this way. The world of entrepreneurs is rough. The last figures I saw reported about a 90% failure rate in the world of entrepreneurship. Even just recently I saw that 94% of ecommerce companies fail within 18 months of their startup. So your chance of success as an entrepreneur is actually pretty slim. If you're going to take that risk and go into that world, there better be a big return at the end of it for you. It has to be more than just owning your own job.

Your business eventually ought to provide you with the ability to generate an above-average lifestyle because your focus as an entrepreneur initially revolves around sustaining the business operations. At some point, there needs to be a reward or you'll get to the end and think, "Why did I do that?". You'll never work so hard in your life as you will when trying to get a business off the ground. You should be rewarded for that work.

Adam: You may as well go work at Costco and call it a day if there's not going to be the opportunity for an above-average reward at some point.

Mike: Right. There's a guy I met years ago. It was the first year I was in business and he was celebrating 25 years of his business. He said when he went into business he went in for a couple of reasons. One was he wanted to make more money. Secondly, he wanted to have more leisure time. Third, he wanted to have a sense of prestige in his community with his relationships. He said he finally figured out after 25 years he had never worked so hard and so much in his life, he had known poverty that he never would have dreamt of and had been humbled beyond his wildest imagination over and over and over.

He told me, "At the end of the day, the one thing I got out of it is I have ultimately turned it into a pretty nice lifestyle, and every single day I come to work, I appreciate the fact that I'm going to face new challenges. So I'm never ever bored.".

At the end of the day, you don't want to have said "I was challenged every day for 30 years but I came out worse off than I went in.". That's not a successful entrepreneur story. Therein lies the need for the three heads of your advisor team.

The first is your legal team to make sure that you're staying safe along the journey, it ends in the way in which you want and your assets are disbursed in the way that you had desired. The second is your accounting and tax team who can make sure that you understand the truth about your business and that you pay an appropriate amount of tax but never more than enough tax. The third is your wealth manager or financial planner to help you accumulate wealth along the way. That wealth accumulation is was allows you an exit plan. Those are the teams and the rationale for them.

Adam: Talk to me about business transitions. What are some key transitions that business owners go through? Are there clear markers or phases in their business that you see?

Mike: No question. The first phase is the startup. Entrepreneurs take the technical skills and they go use those technical skills to basically own their own job. They become their own boss but produce whatever it is that their technical skills are in. Whether you're a self-employed financial planner and you do financial planning, or if you're a carpenter and you open a cabinet shop, or you're a machinist and you open a machine shop, you basically just own your own job at the beginning. You start out being the most technically savvy guy in your company. And that's typically the way companies start.

It could be different for those people that are experienced managers who go in and use their ability to strategize and manage other people and to raise capital. That could be different but, for the most part, the typical entrepreneurial person that we see is a guy who starts off with a technical capability. So it starts off, phase one is they bring the technical expertise and probably not a whole lot else.

One of the reasons why businesses fail is they're not adept in managing their money, in selling, in marketing, in the hiring and utilization of employees. Those are all areas that technicians are often poor at. So one of the things that those who make it through the startup phase have to do is become capable of doing those things that Michael Gerber, who wrote the book called *The E-Myth*, calls the seven elements of management attention.

The seven areas are leadership, finance, strategy, lead generation, lead conversion (which will be sales), customer fulfillment (which is delivering on the promise of whatever you're trying to produce), and then managing your resources. Whatever type of business it is (people, machinery, facilities, technology, etc.) those are the seven areas we talk with clients about in terms of management.

In the second phase, you have to become adept at managing or you have to hire somebody who's adept at it. For those people that are capable of doing at least a satisfactory job on every one of those seven elements, they typically will be able to move to the next level. If you don't get those elements fulfilled, you'll tend to struggle at that point and largely remain involved in trying to produce whatever it is you produce because you can't get out of the technical phase of your business.

To get out of the technical phase and start to become a true entrepreneur and business manager, you've got to be able to put some kind of systems or processes or people into those positions that fulfill at least to some adequate degree those seven elements.

The business generally becomes scalable once that transition is made. If you don't get those done, scalability is difficult. If you do get those done, scalability becomes possible and then it becomes a point of where you're top grading. You're upgrading. You just continue to improve your people, your processes, your equipment, your quality, your customer service, your understanding of customer needs, and you just improve, improve, improve, and as you do, you start to scale up.

In doing so, you can move into that third phase, which is really where you can start to leverage what you know and the systems that are in place to expand your horizons. Maybe you do an acquisition of an ancillary business or you acquire a competitor and integrate that into your business. You can start to leverage the value of assets and knowledge towards exponential growth.

Then the final phase is where you start to make yourself dispensable and where other people are running your operations for you. They're finding the opportunities to expand. They're driving those seven elements of management and you're just overseeing the leadership team.

Those are the four major transitions that an entrepreneur would make to become a mature businessperson. What we say is that you've crossed the chasm that so many businesses don't ever get over and that is becoming scalable to the point where you can enjoy the fruits of continuous growth instead of driving that growth. Becoming scalable is truthfully where one starts to achieve a considerable amount of personal wealth.

Adam: What kind of conversations do you have with the founder and his or her family as they enter into that last phase and begin thinking about exiting their business?

Mike: The question that comes up first is, "Can your business run today without you?". That is the mark of sustainability. Whether anybody admits it or not, the founder is the one who generally sets the standards of how a business operates as well as the quality, the process and the productivity in an organization. My advice when you're going into that fourth phase is to start by validating that all your key processes are accurately documented and then confirm your team members are actually following that documented process as it's described in writing. That way you can continue to produce great results. Once you've documented, then begins the ongoing process of leaning those processes out. In essence, trying to make each process better, faster and cheaper to operate.

Therein lies the freedom to eventually walk away once that gets done and you can prove the results. That's what Ray Krock did with McDonald's. McDonald's didn't go into the hamburger business. He went into the moneymaking business. What he did is figured out the formula that says if you follow my process and follow our quality standards, you can't help but make money. It's called the franchise prototype. If you follow our quality standards, don't screw up our brand and don't deviate from our proven processes, then you will be guaranteed to make money.

How many times have you gone to a restaurant for years and years and love their food. It becomes a local favorite and the guy who owns it is working in the kitchen (or he's the maître d' or whatever). Then he decides to exit that business (whether by choice or not) and sells it to somebody else.

The next guy comes in and has the brainiac idea to take what was a proven history and say, "Let's change the recipes! Let's downgrade the quality. Let's make the portions smaller.". A year later, the business is gone because they deviated from a proven system.

The founder can't do anything about that when that next guy comes on. In order to get top dollar when you leave that business, whether it be through succession or through an exit plan of a sale, the proven ability to say to your successor, "follow our process and you can't help but make money", that is what raises the value of your company.

Secondly, you have to fight the temptation when things are running well to start letting things slip. That includes not becoming cavalier about how your money is spent. For instance, you might get sloppy after a few good years and erode the profits at the end of each year instead of holding some retained earnings. You justify the decision because you say, "Well, this way I don't have to pay so much in taxes.".

By that point in your life, you're making good money and you despise paying taxes. So you begin to justify expenses that, maybe years before, you would have considered frivolous. Instead you say, "Well, I'm either going to pay the Tax Man or we can buy this luxury item.". The problem with that is you just reduced your profitability, which is a key component of selling that business. You will significantly erode the equity value of the business and hurt your future financial security if you do that over a 2, 3, 4, 5-year period. There becomes a real temptation to justify that which the wise entrepreneur will avoid.

Some businesses are less rigidly controlled as time goes on. What I mean is their financial systems are not stellar. Sometimes that's by design so that the owners can pocket the money before it gets reported on the tax return. If you do that, it's a kiss of death. In doing so, you just downgraded the quality of your business, the profitability of your business and the resale-ability of that business. You'll end up saving some taxes but cost yourself a fortune in the resale value of that business. That's a temptation that I hate to see would-be successful founders fall prey to.

There's also another one which is where – this is kind of the opposite of the last example – where a founder gets so rigid in wanting to make sure that he runs up the profitability at the end to sell his business that he lets his operations deteriorate. He cuts staff, he doesn't reinvest in technology or equipment and let's the appearance of the place start to go because doesn't want to invest in maintaining a pristine operation. When a buyer or successor comes there, the business loses curb appeal because the buyer is looking at is the cost of reinvestment. Becoming overly tight-fisted at the end will ultimately detract from the resale value of your company as well.

You have to maintain that business like you're going to run it forever. That means keeping your operations efficient, quality high, reinvesting as appropriate and certainly maintain excellent financial controls that depict an honest and accurate depiction of the financial output of your company. In doing so, it allows the owner to leave on his or her own terms.

If you've got a pristine business with proven value and a proven system for making money in the future, buyers will line up. If you've got a sloppy looking business, an out-of-date business, one that lacks documentation or has unclear (or downright sketchy) financial records then selling it becomes hard. The seller will be forced to discount the price because the buyers rarely are going to overpay. Your business has got to show well under a great exit plan or a succession plan. Even if your successors are internal employees or family members buying out your interest in the company – those people know where all the skeletons are. They're not going to overpay for that business even if they're buying it from mom and dad.

Adam: Those individuals are dangerous to the founder on both sides. A botched succession plan in which someone internal was going to take over and leaves instead means you likely just created the perfect competitor who knows every secret about your business. That is the stuff of nightmares for any business owner.

Mike: Oh sure. That's the other element though I think that's in this. If you're going to look at a succession plan or even an exit plan, make sure that you're communicating with your top people so that they know what's in store for them. Like you said, you do not want to create a competitor on your way out.

Adam: What stories come to mind when you think about each type of transition in which you either saw particularly successful or unsuccessful execution and what was the takeaway?

Mike: Well, we're working on one right now. We're advising a client who's got a significant partner, not a majority, but significant business partner who's retiring. This is a good news/bad news story. Good news story is this is the third time that a senior-level partner has left this business. So there is a track record of success.

One of the things they had done after the first person left was have a partnership agreement put together that was really excellent. It was to define all future transitions where when a partner is going to retire or leave or change directions or in cases where it would be just through involuntary such as a death or disability.

The document they put together was quite good but they have a little bit of a problem. It is very rigid and doesn't take into consideration current changes in the business environment. So it's created more debate than probably necessary. We were hired to help mediate the differences between them to find a reasonable valuation method and valuation system that would supersede the agreement.

There was some difficulty because of the rigidity of it not taking into consideration the new norm but at least they had a road map to work with. They had started the process and then all we've had to do was come in and broaden this as an independent person to bridge the gap on just a couple of issues. Ninety percent of it was predetermined. There wasn't enough latitude or ability to reconcile some differences in that particular agreement to account for changes in the business environment that would have made it unbearable to the remaining partner. We were able to negotiate through it reasonably and got that process done. So that's been a good one.

One of the bad ones, which ended up being a peer, somebody who I did not know but I know of, a young guy, a CPA tax practice. Had a growing business here not too far from us and then he was married and had a couple small children. His wife was no longer working in the business and he had three full-time employees but the business was growing effectively. At 41 years old, he had a heart attack and died.

None of his employees were prepared to know what to do in that event. His wife didn't know what to do in that event. And through a virtual paralysis, business literally just dissolved. Unfortunately, his wife got virtually zero from it because she then had no ability to sell it as a going business. The employees all lost their jobs.

It was a very unfortunate circumstance but I think every business needs to have a plan B. If plan A doesn't work right, for whatever reason, you better have a plan B.

Adam: What should he have done in that situation as you saw it? What would you have suggested he do had you been advising him two years prior to that event?

Mike: He should've had a couple of things. One, he should have had an emergency plan that explained, "If today is my last day and you guys are coming to work tomorrow and I'm not, this is what you do, this is how you handle it, and this is who's going to be making the decisions, and this is how you're going to tell our clients, and this is who to call to find a buyer. In the meantime, here's a list of my attorney. Here's a peer or a colleague that you can call that'll help bridge the gap until that happens, somebody that is a friend of our firm that will help us or buy it.".

I have a relationship with a guy who has a business model very similar to mine. We have a gentleman's agreement that we would step in in the event if something happened to one of us, the other would step in to help bridge the gap either to acquire the practice and take care of the family or to assist them temporarily until a buyer could be identified to help make sure that we're in good shape.

Our current emergency plan also has a list of advisors that have agreed to act as a governing board in the event that something would happen to me. Upon my untimely demise, they would provide some additional support and horsepower to our team. In addition, our internal team means we already have successors in place if something happens to me.

You've got give somebody the ability to come unlock the door the next day and answer the phone if something happens to you as the business owner. An emergency plan is at the very least a partnership plan, preferably a contingency plan and, at the very least, an emergency plan. It's no different than what you would do if your computer systems went down. You must have an answer in that case of how your company gets back up and running the next day. That's just part of being a good businessperson.

Again, in most entrepreneurial businesses, the guy at the top is the single most important person, not only with the customer relationships but with creditor relationships as well. That's part of a good emergency plan. Your creditors or your banker knows who your key people are and have some trust that you're going to make it and they're going to be able to collect even if you're not there.

Adam: Beyond the internal value of it, a well-written emergency plan can also become part of your message to clients as well. Most customers of a service business or a long-term business want to know what happens if something happens to you. It becomes a differentiator between you and the guy or girl down the street when you can say, "We thought through these things. We take care of our own business and I'm going to take care of yours.". There's value in it from a sales perspective as well that makes investing time in emergency planning worthwhile.

Mike: Well, I'm sure you've been asked the question in your own practice. I've been asked it hundreds of times. Clients will say, "We're entrusting you to help us with our finances. What happens if something happens to you? Who steps in?". That's why they want to meet the people on your team.

Adam: Exactly.

Mike: That's one thing I try am constantly working, particularly at this stage in my life. I'm not looking to leave any time soon, but at 62 years old, it's important to make sure that I don't do a lot of meetings by myself. I need to have somebody else in those meetings so that the client has a sense of depth and our staff has an understanding of what each client's about. I try to be intentional about that. I'm not successful 100% of the time but at least I try to do a good job of introductions to the rest of our staff. Going back to the story I shared earlier, that other professional was 41 years old and had a massive heart attack. Surely, I don't wish that on anybody but I think it's something everybody needs to be prepared for.

Adam: Absolutely. It does happen.

Mike: It does.

Adam: Have you ever personally been involved in one of the three types of transitions we talked about as far as a sale, a succession, or a cessation? Did you ever try to buy another practice and what did you learn from it?

Mike: I have attempted to buy a couple of practices in the past. It comes down to the fact that the business that we're in is very relational. It's face to face and so the sellers are usually cautious. I think I've learned from each one. We've looked at three practices to buy over the last few years. Two of them looked like they would be good fits. One was not. We decided not to provide an offer or a letter of intent. The other two we did.

Ultimately, one was withdrawn for sale and the other one was sold to another company because they were fearful of a perceived liability of our providing both wealth management services and accounting services. They believed in the old model of accountancy I mentioned earlier. They felt that our ability to provide wealth management was not an asset but, rather, was almost a violation of their core belief that accounting people only need to be accounting people and that they shouldn't get into something where they would earn income from financial services. As much as we tried to convince that person that we were ultimately a good fit, it didn't work.

I had a business partner when I first started out and we split that partnership up after seven years. That one actually did go very smoothly. We had a partnership agreement when we first started in the business and it held instructions on a variety of different methods to separate our business. We just implemented that when we finally decided to go our separate ways. The whole thing took about an hour to separate our business. It was a very easy to do and, within the span of a month, I had moved out from the old location we shared and acquired a new spot.

That was largely successful because we had the business designed around our relationships with our clients. I had relationships with my clients. He had relationships with his and there wasn't a lot of co-mingling between us. As far as the rest of all the equipment and technology, that was pretty easy to replicate and replace. But it was the relationships that could have been messier. Since we eventually decided to base the division of our clients according to who had which relationships, it actually went pretty simple in our case.

Adam: Was that determined in the partnership agreement beforehand, or was that something you

came up when it become clear you were going to part ways?

Mike: It actually came up when we decided we were going to part ways. The partnership agreement was written with the assumption that somebody was going to leave the business. Since neither of us were going to get out of the business, there was a gap in the partnership agreement that needed to be addressed. We agreed quickly on that method and then the chips were going to fall where they may.

I was fortunate that I ended up with a significant amount of the business. That is actually what really generated the desire to end the partnership to begin with. My staff and I handled about 2/3 of all the clients and revenue. Yet, we weren't being compensated for the fact that we were working significantly more hours than my ex-partner and his staff. The split became inevitable once we both realized that was happening.

I was able to re-launch pretty effectively with my team and move quickly. We had also had a very good customer support through the transition and did a very good job of communication with our clients about what we were doing, why we were doing it and what they can expect with the change. Our goal was to take away any guesswork for them and minimize uncertainty.

By doing that, we were able to get virtually 100% conversion rate. Actually, we had two other clients move over whom we had done a significant amount of work for but were not the primary contact at the time the partnership split. We had a couple of those clients move over to us as well. So my ex-partner and I decided we would make a choice initially as to whose clients were whose but, at the end of the day, it was always the client's choice. So it really wasn't that difficult. Any partnership split it going to be pandemonium to go through because there's just a lot of moving parts. It ended up being the right thing to do in our case and we've had no regrets in doing it.

Adam: What suggestions do you have for someone considering one of the three paths in terms of an exit transition? We've talked about the need to have processes documented and the need to have an emergency plan in place before then. What other counsel do you have for someone who comes to you and says, "Mike, I'm thinking of retiring / selling / transferring my business to my kids. What do I need to do?".

Mike: I think fundamentals are where it all starts. Consider how you can make your business attractive to somebody who would want to be an absentee owner. That's a good reference point. Think about what the business would need to be attractive to someone who wants to invest his or her money, doesn't want to work in the business but wants it to continue to go on profitably and produce a return on investment. That's the ultimate succession plan for you as a business owner because, in that case, you don't ever have to find a buyer because you've replaced yourself with a team. Therein lies the path to building solid fundamentals in your business.

Begin to view your business as an investment and examine what it would have to be like if you were the one looking at it from an investment standpoint. That obviously highlights the need for high levels of accountability and reporting capabilities that let you know everything going on with every metric and financial condition you can have. Your financial system needs to generate useful information so that an absentee owner could simply monitor it from afar. I think that's the best possible scenario.

The next owner's expectation for return on investment is much different if he's just going to be investing his money versus if he's investing his money and he has to come over and take over your job. That's a completely different type of buyer. If you could find somebody that says, "I'm going to buy it. We're going to take the vice president and he's now president, and we're just going to keep moving on with what we're doing", that's the best possible outcome.

So again, I think fundamentals are the key starting point. Getting the business in a position where the owner could say, "I'm going to take the next three months off.", walk out the door that same day and come back to find it's still running well is the ultimate Litmus test for a business that is ready for a sale at its highest possible price. I would do that if I were the one considering a sale.

Specifically, I would make sure my key performance indicators (KPIs) are on the mark, that we're hitting at least industry averages or better and our tax returns reflect that we're profitable. Those three things go a long way in validating your value proposition. Also, I would say it's imperative to make sure your credit accounts with others are pristine, that you have good relationships with them and that you have a good payment history. If you want to sour a deal as quickly as possible, have your primary supplier tell a prospective buyer that you're notorious for paying 30 days late. That's a red flag. So those kinds of things have to be scrutinized and addressed before moving toward a sale.

The other thing is to make sure your customers are paying on time and you don't have a collection problem. Buyers are not enamored to think, "I've got to come in and fight with my customers to get paid? Not really interested in that.". Think about how to turn your business into one that clearly communicates, "This is an easy business to run because it all works.". Every component has to work well from the financials, the quality of the products, the customer referral levels to the customer satisfaction levels. It's essential to be able to provide to a seller is customer satisfaction and/or a list of your referral rates. Those should be a part of your core metrics that are being tracked on a regular basis.

Those are the kind of things that can do more to instill confidence in your buyer than anything you possibly say. If the money's there, the customers are coming, the business is growing, and long term trends are good, you can't help but have somebody be interested in buying that business. Those are the things I'd be looking at.

Adam: Is there anything else that we haven't talked about that you want to make sure gets included in this conversation?

Mike: The only other thing I can think of is make sure your company is multigenerational. That is, you need to have some people that are seasoned, some people that are in the mid part of their career and some people at the early part of their career. That demonstrates you're leaving your buyer a company that's got promise and the people that work there see that there's opportunity and value for them to stay. There's opportunity for a career. There's opportunity for growth. There's opportunity for engagement within learning new things and challenging themselves and to introduce new opportunities within that business. I think being multigenerational is really critical.

Also, make sure your company is a place that is fun to work in. At the end of the day, we all spend so much time doing this, if you're not having a fun time, why do it? Work to make sure that your culture is diverse, it's energized, it's fun, that you have people that want to come to work most days. If it's a great place to be, the odds are they'll want to give their best and they'll want to learn new things.

That's a whole lot better than having to cajole, and beg them to push themselves for the organization. They'll do it because it's part of their DNA. Those are the kind of things I'd be looking at. I think cultural fit is something people don't take enough into consideration but it's becoming more and more important to buyers. If someone's looking at acquiring you and integrating you into their existing business, they will be asking how well it's going to fit culturally with their organization. It can be one of the more difficult elements to evaluate but also can be one of the most important and valuable.

Adam: Yeah, those intangibles will get you if you're not paying attention to.

Mike: That's for sure.

Adam: Mike, I really appreciate your input on this and the time.

Mike: My pleasure.

Chapter 14: Victor Pressier - Victor Pressier Acclaimed Author, Executive Coach and Mentor to Ultra-high Net Worth Families.

Vic has spent the past 10 years as an Executive Coach and Mentor to Heirs. As co-author of the books *Preparing Heirs* and *Philanthropy, Heirs & Values* and the soon to be released *Family Meetings*, he is a recognized specialist in advising closely held or family-controlled businesses.

A former Resident Professor of Management at the University of the Pacific, Vic has taught at the graduate school level in Strategic Planning and Organizational Development. His most recent work has been with The Williams Group, where he is the Managing Director (and minority owner) of the nation's oldest and largest Coaching organization. His primary responsibility with The Williams Group is the oversight of management succession and personal development plans for likely heirs of closely held major businesses.   In the course of this work he is one of the three founders of The Institute for Preparing Heirs, located in Pasadena, CA where he now resides.

Prior to the above, with the help of Lehman Brothers, he conducted a leveraged buyout of companies from Allied Products of Chicago. He has served as President of Litton Industries Great Lakes Division (shipbuilding, ship repairs, fleet operations, marine architectural design), and sold the Litton Group to

George Steinbrenner (then with Kinsman Marine, his family owned company). He was the first appointed Railway Official to be assigned responsibility for on-site analysis of railroad collisions and derailments working for the Chicago & NorthWestern Railway, under the leadership of Ben W. Heineman, and negotiated new industry insurance arrangements with Lloyds of London.

More recently, Vic has served as CEO of Networked Picture Systems in Santa Clara CA, where he served as Board Chair, taking the company public with an IPO. Later, it was taken private by an English company. He also served as an onsite representative for a group of investors who held a major financial position in a food product distribution/wholesaler in the San Francisco Bay area...a major supplier for numerous private grocers in the area. As CEO of FindLaw, a high-tech web-based legal information service, Vic negotiated its sale to WestLaw of Canada. He now serves as Board Chairman or Board Member of closely held family-controlled corporations in the United States.

Vic served in the US Army Infantry for 3 years, was honorably discharged with the rank of Sergeant, earned his B.S. in Physical Sciences from Stanford (Summa Cum Laude) and his MBA from Stanford. He has 3 grown sons and 3 grandchildren, and lives in Pasadena, CA with his wife, Diane.

The following conversation took place on February 9, 2016 Between Vic Pressier and Adam Broughton, CFP®.

Here's What We Talk About:

- What exactly does a family dynamics coach do?
- What do the statistics say about how prepared business owners typically are for a major transition?
- What is the #1 concern the ultra high net worth couples typically have about the wealth they've accumulated?
- How should founders handle conflict between what their kids want and what they want to have happen with the business?
- What two most important components are most critical to emphasize if a founder wants to maximize their chances of transition success?
- Plus a whole lot more so read on!

Adam: Vic, it's a pleasure to have you with me and I appreciate your input. Can you share with me what is so important about family coaching and why it's worth the time and effort required to do it well?

Vic: Thanks, Adam. First, let me say I'm profoundly convinced that one of the most important things a professional advisor can bring to a family is to teach them to think appropriately about the transition. That means the heirs, the beneficiaries, the trustees all need to first come to a place where they accept that a change needs to take place. The status quo cannot and will not continue forever.

The ability to do that requires the professional to be much broader in experience than just an attorney, just a CPA, just an insurance guy. Most professionals never "leave their lane" of experience and simply focus on the technical aspects of their role. They aren't comfortable starting conversations about legacy or family succession planning because they either know it's a potential minefield or they just don't have confidence they'll end up with a positive result. However, that leaves the family exposed to potential risk even though it protects the professional advisor.

Let's take the CPA for example. If everything is designed in a transition around tax efficiency, you are potentially giving up operating and learning flexibility for kids. It may not even be the case that tax efficiency is the primary objective of the family. In that case, establishing a rigid tax structure around the succession plan leaves the whole thing at risk of failure. So you have to be very careful to look at the whole transition, not just the financial aspects of it.

Adam: When did you come to that realization? Was there a specific event in your career where it dawned on you that you had been doing it incorrectly or other people had and you decided to start doing it this way?

Vic: The heirs I was encountering made it apparent they needed something different than what they were getting. When we completed a transition and followed up with the heirs afterwards, the heirs would say things like, "My gosh, just so we could be 3% more tax efficient, I'm now unable to complete this other merger that is a real opportunity for us.".

Other times I heard, "Well, my gosh just because we placed it in a trust, I cannot make an acquisition except back into the trust. I now can't benefit from the end result of the acquisition unless the trustee approves everything. All these devices to create tax efficiency – I feel just like a horse that's been hobbled at night out on the prairie. I can't wander very far, can I?". It was the heirs who educated me on this need for a broader scope and the need for a family coach to be involved in the estate and transition planning upfront.

Adam: What kind of research did you do into that as you started to hone in on your process?

Vic: The research was really done with the families in the field. I worked with The Williams Group for years and The Williams Group has experience with tracking more than 3,000 families through their transition. To those families that succeeded, they asked, "What's different between you and the other families that didn't succeed?". The results consistently showed that families who were successful had a pattern of trust and communication within their family. That pattern was established *before* the transition happened in their business or family.

Adam: You mentioned business transitions. What are some key phases that you see family businesses go through as they move toward an eventual succession?

Vic: I'm not going to say all family businesses or only the successful or failed transitions go like this but here's a scenario I often see take place. The transition starts off with the founder's doctor or physician telling him, "Harry, you can't keep up 60-hour weeks. You have to think about transition.". That starts the whole thing rolling.

From there, they go to the lawyer and say, "What's the structure to make this transition occur? I want to leave most of it to my kids but I want to have enough for my wife and I left to live on. We've got to be sure we won't ever have to rely on the kids or the government for our lifestyle.". And from that point, it spreads out.

The lawyer then gets involved and says something like, "Well, we can handle the tax costs by using insurance properly. We can handle a lot of the tax issues by having a CPA gather and pull together certain assets in a certain configuration; limited partnership, whatever. We can shield you further by putting in a structure of a trust.". About this time, the owner is sitting there, nodding his head, and says, "Yes, yes, let's do that!". The attorney then starts drafting documents, the documents get signed, trusts get funded, and insurance gets bought. Nobody really knows exactly what they just did but now they can say it's done.

That conversation is distinctly missing a fundamental question: What would work best for the kids? That's where the trouble starts because 70% of transitions fail following the transition to the heirs. Seven in every ten transitions fail and that's been true for at least the last 100 years.

Adam: In my experience, highly successful business owners often tend to be type-A personalities. I can see how the focus immediately can turn to making a plan; executing and getting it done once they realize they need to make a change. What are some of the questions that you help them think through or that you ask to help them take a step back before they start charging down the strategy path?

Vic: Well, I first ask them what their ultimate wish is for the future of what they have built. They're pretty comfortable saying it. They usually say three things: "First, I'd like to take care of Mom and I for the rest of our lives and be sure of that. I'd like my kids to successfully build a legacy of their own. I want the family to remain unified and coherent and love one another and be happy.". Those are the big three.

Adam: I can just see a conversation like that going so many different directions. I'm thinking through a couple of the families that I work with whom we're trying to start those conversations with. One example right now is two cousins who are actually the second-generation owners of their business and they don't necessarily see eye to eye. They have kids who are different ages and they seem to want different things for their children and how they want their kids to be able to engage with the business. What would you suggest as far as bringing them to the same side of the table? How do you bridge a gap like that when you know that they don't agree on what's most important?

Vic: I've never met the folks you're talking about but the answer is real simple. This was laid on me like a ton of bricks about ten years ago when I was working with a family in a similar situation. In that instance I asked them,

"Why don't you have the children develop an estate plan for you? Ask them to develop an estate plan that meets the three criteria I just described. #1 – It has to take care of each of you financially for the rest of our life. #2 – It has to provide for the ongoing success of the business. #3 - If they do it together, it'll be something that keeps this next generation coherent as a family and not fussing and fighting.

I told them to have their kids develop the plan with the family's advisors and present it to Mom and Dad. Meet Mom and Dad's needs first using their advisors and the knowledge those advisors have of the assets in play. It's an astoundingly simple approach that has a great downstream impact.

Adam: Have you found that that creates a conflict of interest to have the kids be setting the plan for the parents while they're trying to meet their own goals? How does the plan turn out?

Vic: No, the biggest problem is the lawyers. The lawyers will say, "Oh my gosh, it's Mom and Dad who are my client. How can I serve you too?". That's when you have to get into the education process with the lawyers and say, "Look, here's an agreement. Here are five or six of the largest law firms in the United States and here's how they handle that. *The family is the client, not the individual.*". They typically respond, "Oh, I see.".

Executing a new agreement serving the client family is a transition in the thought process for them. If someone passes away in the family, we don't lose our client because now our client is the entire family. Suddenly there's a pathway opened up. Every law firm wants to retain their client.

Adam: Thinking about that concept of an advisory team, I call them their success team. Who would you say are the most critical people to have in the conversation on the success team?

Vic: Obviously, it's got to be both the parents and the heirs and their spouses... all together, all in the same room at the same time, and (hopefully) led by a trusted advisor to make certain all voices get heard!

Adam: Which professional advisors do you suggest are in on these conversations? And at what point do you bring each one in in the process?

Vic: There's no question that you have to have the family's legal, accounting and insurance and overall estate plan advisors present. But they can only be present *after* the family has reached consensus on the following question: *What is the mission for your family's wealth.*

What is your mission statement? I'm not talking about your business statement. I'm talking about the mission for the family's wealth. And by wealth, I am not only referring to your assets, your liquid assets and your property assets. I'm talking about your name, your reputation, your faith, your relations in the community and your philanthropy. That's what constitutes your wealth. *What is the mission that you all agree upon for that wealth?*

Once you've done that, you have to develop a glossary of terms for the family that explains each element that is addressed in that mission. Only then does the family & trusted advisor turn it over to the success team and say, "Now, we're going to go ahead with our plan. Your new client is the family and we do not want you to propose items in conflict with this mission. If you've already drawn up a plan before we had agreed upon the Family Wealth Mission Statement, you ought to be able to tell us whether it conflicts with this family mission. We need to know about it now and your proposed plan needs to be altered because the mission drives the mechanics, not vice versa.".

Adam: That's so key – the idea of the mission driving the mechanics. It's profound and, unfortunately, it tends to be the other way around where there's nobody asking those questions. What usually happens is the family is lost in a quagmire of strategies and advisors saying, "Well, we could do this or we could do that. How do we decide?". Advisors are can present ideas but if there's no consensus on what the family mission is, how can you reach an agreement on which strategy is the best fit for the goals?

Vic: That's where the necessity for a Most Trusted Advisor comes into play. First of all, these inheritance/estate ideas start getting drawn up as soon as the business is large enough for the family to be concerned. It has nothing to do whether they have children or not. Secondly, a lot of times the structure is being laid out for purposes of management, taxes, and ownership rather than alignment with the family's mission. Now, having done that, as the kids mature, they begin to have their own wishes whether or not they are involved in the family business. At that point and time, you have to look back and start saying, ooh, we need to try to figure out now how to untangle what's been created.

A great little story I always give is of when Mr. Smith got remarried. His new bride brought four children to the marriage and he brought four children to the marriage. They were in agreement and decided they would divide their estate in eight ways. Two years later, astoundingly, the woman became pregnant. It was the first child between the two of them. Bursting with pride, they were able to announce this to their eight blended-family children and say, "We now have to make the adjustments to each. Instead of getting 1/8, you'll get 1/9. Of course, the estate has grown but you'll each get 1/9 of the entire estate.". The kids unanimously rejected the proposal. They said, "We are not going to share with this new unknown child of yours. We will not cooperate in adjusting the estate which is in trust.".

Stunned, the parents had to set up a whole separate trust fund and estate to make sure that ninth child had a proportional inheritance. If your kids are not involved in the planning, it's very tough to say when are you going to have to go back and re-examine. The laws will change in this country, the tax rates will change, the permissiveness of estates and trusts will adjust so you've got to have the flexibility to make changes and unity within the family about the overall mission.

Adam: We've talked about trust and communication laying the foundation for any kind of successful transition. I'm sure you have plenty of examples, but could you provide an example of somebody and the specific circumstances leading up to the transition and what happened afterwards in a case where it both did not work out and then in a case where it just worked wonderfully? Is there any one that's particularly close to your heart?

Vic: Oh yeah, but let me give you just a couple of facts first. The Williams Group interviewed over 3000 families that had transitioned over a period of 20 years. On the back cover of the book *Preparing Heirs*, you'll see quotes from families that we've served like the Hewlett family, the Coors family, etc. They don't have to all be big leaguers but those are a few names you'll recognize.

Here are the important two facts you really have to keep in mind that we learned through the interviews. First, when the last parent passes on, over 90% of all financial accounts are moved to a new financial advisor. Period. Over 90% percent move on because the kids don't know the advisors, never met them and don't know what the advisors did for the family. Over 90% of the accounts move. They're lost. They're gone. They're at another firm. Second, over 70% of large estates fail or are significantly depleted in the transition following the second spouse's death. That means the assets and/or the family harmony is lost or dissipated. They get burned up in litigation, disputes, bad judgment, etc. Over 70% of all the estates fail.

Now I'll give you the top three reasons they fail. The great majority of those estates fail because of a breakdown of trust and communication _within the family_. The second largest contributor, 25% of the failures, is _heirs are not prepared for the responsibility that is suddenly thrust upon them_. The third biggest cause is _there does not exist in the family a consensus to what the family wealth exists for_. Is it to serve them? Is it to serve the community? Is it to provide liquidity? Whatever it is, there is no consensus.

Less than 3% of the post-transition failures – _less than 3%_ – are due to professional mistakes. So, if you're a family advisor and you're worried about whether you did a good job for this family, what are you going to worry about? Your professional work? Your signatures? The failure to file or the proper entity structure? No. You very rarely make a mistake once you've reached a certain level of expertise in your profession as an advisor, CPA, lawyer, etc. Where the mistakes are made are _within the family_ as they prepare for the transition. Those are the facts. That's why the need for the kind of things you do and helping your clients address questions like how success teams should work, whom they should consist of, and where their focus should be. That's why that kind of work that you're doing is so doggone important. It's critical to the long-term success of families who deal with it.

Adam: Well, thanks Vic. I really appreciate your insight and time on the interview.

Chapter 15: Bryan Feller, President, National Christian Foundation of California

Bryan Feller was an unlikely executive. He set his sights during college on becoming a pastor and obtained his undergraduate degree in Theology. However, he soon found he had a gift for marketing and strategy as a result of the help he received from several early mentors. He ultimately decided to keep the faith and stay in business rather than becoming a pastor.

Bryan got his MBA and was instrumental in leading several companies to double-digit growth. He led one company to make the Inc. 500 list of fastest growing companies twice. He started a consulting firm in 2005 focused on marketing strategy and sales force development. Bryan has worked with nearly 50 organizations as a consultant and coach ranging from start-ups to Fortune 500 companies across the United States.

Bryan is currently President of the National Christian Foundation of California (NCF). NCF allows high capacity givers to obtain greater tax advantages from their giving. They specialize in cases of non-liquid gifts like stock, real estate, and closely held business interests. NCF has facilitated over $4 billion in grants to thousands of churches, ministries, and nonprofits.

Bryan married his high school sweetheart, Becky. They are now "empty-nesters" with two children, Westley and Courtney, and live in Riverside, CA.

The following interview took place on December 5, 2015 between Bryan Feller and Adam Broughton, CFP®.

Here's What We Talk About:

- Why should charitable planning be part of every business transition plan even if a business owner has never given a dollar to anyone before?
- What are a few of the biggest mistakes you've seen founders make in the months and years leading up to a transition?
- How far in advance of the founder's exit should the transition planning process start?
- Plus a whole lot more so read on!

Adam: Hi Bryan. Can you give my readers an overview of your professional background and how you got to where you are now?

Bryan: Yeah, I thought I was going to be a pastor – I got a degree in theology and didn't end up going that direction in the end. I ended up in a marketing role and loved it. So I got an MBA and stayed in sales and marketing. I started my own consulting company in 2005. It was mostly marketing strategy and then that kind of evolved into a lot of sales force development consulting. We kind of landed in with the larger Fortune 500 space in terms of our clientele and did really well until about 2009. Then we did not so well.

The company closed up and I did some interim CEO work for a while after that. National Christian Foundation (NCF) actually ended up being a client of mine. Through some transactions that I helped them close, I just ended up staying there because I loved it. I felt like I was working with the same people I had been working with before in my own company in terms of business owners. It was all the same things they were thinking about just with a charitable and social impact focus.

I loved NCF because I don't think I would do well in a fundraising role, and, fortunately, NCF doesn't do fundraising (even though most people think we do). We're essentially generous giving consultants. We're generous givers ourselves and so it's been a lot of fun connecting with what charitable people are doing. I'm also honored getting to know their businesses intimately and making all those other connections between business owners work. That's kind of the short version for me.

Adam: In your current role with NCF, can you describe a little bit about how do business owners find you and what are you talking with them about as you build a relationship?

Bryan: A lot of our business comes from introductions although I am doing a lot more speaking at ministry events. Very rarely does anyone come to us and say, "Whom should we give to?". They're usually coming to us already having been connected to some kind of charity that they're passionate about. If we can connect with them through that charity, that's always a good thing. Of course, professional advisors are a great source of referrals for us. Folks that are having charitable conversations with their clients refer people to us on a regular basis. That's how we get into the conversation.

I run the California chapter of NCF and the tax code in California is one of the most repressive in the country for business owners. The value proposition of NCF, at least in California, is there are almost always easily implementable strategies to be generous if you understand the tax structure. I'm not talking about just leaving your state after death. I mean right now while you're living. In particular, there's a breed of business owner that are what I would call the "50%

club" people. That means you're giving away 50% of your Adjusted Gross Income (AGI) each year.

When my wife and I had our business, there were a couple of years we were at that level of giving 50% of our AGI but we're not there right now. We aspire to be there because we know the needs having been on a ministry team full time in the past ourselves. We believe what we have was God's and, if we have extra, it wasn't to ramp up our lifestyle. A lot of those people tend to gravitate to NCF because NCF really provides a lot of tools for them to be a lot more tax efficient in their giving then they could be just by using a simple donor advised fund or foundation.

Adam: That's excellent. Those are the types of people who I come across who tend to be in the second half of their business life in terms of the business lifecycle. You have startup mode where people are just trying to survive initially and everything is held together with duct tape pretty much, and then they get several years under their belt as a business owner and actually start breaking even (Phase 1). Then they've got cash flow coming in, they start expanding and sometimes raise more capital (phase 2). Eventually, the business really starts to grow and they hit their peak earning years (Phase 3). That's when I get introduced to a lot of my clients.

That's also when they start to feel more of that tax bite. They don't tend to be particularly charitable at that stage. The conversations are more motivated by they want their tax bill to shrink and they want to be able to keep more of what they're making. At some point the conversation starts to shift in their later years and they start thinking more toward legacy (Phase 4). Part of that conversation is about retiring and what they're going to do when they have nothing else to do. That's when more of those philanthropic things come in for my clients. Either at that point or if they suddenly have an opportunity to sell a going business concern and they find out how much tax they're going to have to pay if they sell it without any advanced planning.

Bryan: Yeah, that sounds about right.

Adam: In your experience, what are a few of the mistakes that you've seen business owners make in the third and fourth phases as they begin thinking about making a transition either to retirement or selling their business? Are there things you've encountered that are common missteps business owners make that end up hurting their business or taking them away from their goals?

Bryan: Gosh, for us, when people plan in advance to sell their business, those are the easiest folks to deal with. Most of the tragedies are the folks that got excited about the prospect of a sale and didn't have anybody on their advisory team to walk with them through it. They just had to find a buyer quickly or they suddenly found a buyer so they went from zero to 100 just because someone offered to write them a check. It could be the case their business wasn't all that marketable and they were just happy to get out.

The problem is that transition happens so quickly they really didn't think through it and they missed an opportunity. They pay huge capital gains on their stock because they just jump into a sale without planning. It happens even with folks who are otherwise generous too. They jump into a sale without anyone there to ask the question of how charitable giving or generosity could play a role in that transaction. They end up paying tax and having less money to be generous with after the sale.

I also encounter people that have planned for a long time but then, when it comes time to execute, they just get excited or a deal comes along and they decide it has to be right now. I understand all the reasons why that happens. Selling business is a big deal. It's not like you have buyers lined up to buy your business most of the time.

So, when you do find a buyer, it's tempting to just jump in. What I also see is people have either only have a CPA or there are just holes in their success team. They don't really have anybody who knows anything about charitable tax law and so it's not even a part of the conversation. It's sad when we get called after they've already completed a transition and there's nothing that we can really do.

That is the single biggest mistake and we literally see it every week. Every week I hear about someone that sold a business, they are generous in other areas of their life but they weren't able to be charitable in the sale of the business because they didn't know or they didn't have the right person on the team to ask the right questions. Actually, just last week we had another one come up.

Adam: What happened? Tell me about it. How did that conversation go?

Bryan: This one was somebody that a church referred to us. They were going to make a million dollar gift and they had a business they were selling. So I got in touch with the donor to see how we could help. What was sad is we figured out quickly this person actually was aware of the strategy I would have recommended. They knew another business owner who had used the strategy effectively. This person who was referred to me had previously sold another business without any planning and wanted to sell this one the right way by giving before the sale. But, again, they got into I wouldn't say a panic but they just got into –

Adam: "Go mode".

Bryan: Yeah, they just went into Go Mode and also they had pre-conceived notions about what could and couldn't be done that weren't accurate.

Adam: What was the error in their logic in that case?

Bryan: The majority shareholder was an atheist and the person I had been referred to only owned 25% of the stock. My client was a minority shareholder and he assumed the atheist wouldn't agree to allow them to give shares ahead of time to a faith-based organization. However, there were a number of things that could've been done. One was to gift the shares to NCF and then buy them back with the next day. They could have brought them back on an installment note and created an ongoing gift or a deferred gift. The point is there were some creative things that we could've done to mitigate the majority shareholder's fears about a third party involved in the transaction. There could have been a lot of things that we could have done but we just didn't have the time. The transaction was too far down the road by the time we got involved.

Adam: What kind of a time window should a business owner give him or herself if they're going to explore any kind of philanthropic strategy as it relates to a business transition? When is it too late (other than after the check is signed)?

Bryan: Well, it's better to start the planning in the first half of the year if possible. Half of our revenue comes in December and a lot of that has to do with people trying to wrap up all their tax affairs by December 31. There are a lot of people involved in the sale of a business – an appraisal is often required, there are a lot of lawyers involved, there are often trusts that need to be setup, etc. If you try to ram that into the fourth quarter, we may be able to get it through but it can limit your options. That's why, if you're going to do a transaction like that, it's better to try to wrap it up by the end of the third quarter because there's so much to do. There can be a ton of lawyering that has to happen, environmental studies to complete and sometimes multiple appraisals. It's a pretty long list of things that need to happen when you're selling a business. Adding a layer of charitable planning on short notice tends to mess things up. My rule of thumb is make sure it happens in third quarter. There's so much that can go wrong if you wait until fourth quarter with all of your team, not just on NCF's side.

I'll tell you a second story about somebody who did it wrong. It was with a piece of real estate but the same principle applies. This was a couple of weeks ago, maybe a month ago. A guy did a $100,000 gift to a capital campaign in his church. The stewardship pastor at the church was doing a happy dance because they got a six-figure gift. However, we knew the gentleman and we knew how the gift happened. The guy paid $100,000 in taxes that he didn't have to in order to make that gift. He liquidated a piece of real estate in a really bad way. The irony was people were doing a happy dance not realizing the guy would have easily doubled that gift had he had an advisor that told him how to give it properly. It was the same principle. He didn't give before the transaction of the real estate. He gave after tax. It's just one of a hundred of those stories where the outcome could have been better for everyone if someone had been there to ask the right questions.

Adam: Let's say you have a business owner who is generous but they also need to retain a bulk of the money they expect to receive from the sale of their business to support their future lifestyle indefinitely. Is there still room for philanthropic planning for someone who isn't really thinking they're going to give the whole thing away?

Bryan: Absolutely. In fact, that's the whole point. Rarely do I ever see somebody that gives the whole thing away. An example of one strategy I use a lot is to gift some nonvoting shares of the business to a donor advised fund before the sale. That may only amount to 10% of the total value. When the sale happens, the money that's going from those shares can avoid capital gains taxes as long as it's done properly. That's where the savings comes from. It's a deduction to offset the tax owed on the income received by the business owner on the sale. You can also gift your whole business into your giving fund and then buy it back. Or your kids could buy it back on a note. There are a lot of different strategies available even when the business owners don't intend to give it all away. It's when people make assumptions about what can and can't be done that problems occur. Assumptions and mistakes go hand in hand when it comes to planning.

The reality is most people don't give their whole business. Most people give a small piece and there are a lot of strategies NCF uses every day to make sure that those kinds of things go well. I'll give one more example even though I know you don't want the conversation to get lost in technical jargon. What we've also done is put some of the shares into a separate LLC. In that case, that person designed the LLC so he maintained complete control. The shares were nonvoting and could be bought back at any time. It was a really flexible strategy and made it easy to give any amount of shares of the company stock into your giving fund before a sale.

We're working with somebody right now who's giving 15% of his stock and he doesn't plan on selling for 10 years. He doesn't have a buyer in mind yet but he's maxing out his deductions. He's in the 50% club. He's doing some of his giving using those nonvoting shares in the LLC to make regular distributions through a charitable shareholder. He's using the same strategy as outlined above even though his intent is not to sell right away. It's an easy strategy to give shares ahead of time even if it's just a small percentage of the business.

Adam: That would check a lot of boxes for a lot of people because they're not giving up control in that case. That also means not having to make too many major decisions at one time but still being able to maximize your deductions. It provides an additional tax management tool while the founder is still running his or her business to help both accumulate personal wealth. It also means he or she keeps more of what they have while still creating a charitable impact and working on their legacy. It just sounds like that creates a lot of flexibility and another tool in the box, so to speak, as they're looking to grow their personal wealth and be generous. Basically, doing well and doing good.

Bryan: Yeah, plus you get to take a huge deduction upfront for those shares. Let's say you give – well, the guy in the example is going to give 15% of this company. He's going to take a large tax deduction that he can carry forward for six years. That's going to allow him to actually free-up cash that would otherwise have gone to pay taxes that he can now use to give more. So it's a really great strategy.

Adam: Earlier in the book, I described the three main categories of exit strategies as either a sale involving an outside buyer, a succession involving an internal buyer, or a cessation, which would be just collecting your receivables and calling it a day. As you think about those categories, do any stories come to mind that you've seen in which you saw someone do it well or particularly fail in any one of those?

Bryan: I run into all of them. I'm just trying to think of the most pertinent story. I'll use an example of the succession plan when you're moving your assets down a generation. If the person's entire intent is to move all of their assets, they're going to pay a lot of taxes. I ran across a story the other day in which this gentleman had a $30 million cash reserve set aside to pay his estate tax liability. We were able to get that to zero. Now, a person is 100% intent on 100% of their assets passing to kids for an estate that size, they're probably not going to get it to zero. It's going to be difficult to realize any meaningful savings. However, if you're charitable in the process, there are a lot of ways to get all that estate tax liability down to zero (or at least close to it). If people develop a generous, philanthropic mindset with their advisors or can at least be open to it, they'll usually find creative (and legal) ways to accomplish their goals. If it's just about passing assets to kids though, everybody's going to pay a lot of taxes.

Adam: I run into people who think there is some mystical trick that only the super rich know that allows them to avoid paying tax. That's just false (at least in terms of anything that's actually legal). The truth is there are only three choices of where your money ultimately goes. It's the three G's of legacy planning. It's either going to be God - meaning charitable giving - Granny - meaning a family member - or the Government – meaning taxes. That's it. Those are the only choices you have. You can decide who gets which piece of the pie if you do some planning.

Bryan: Yeah, that definitely rings true.

Adam: What specific suggestions for someone who is in that zone between 5 and 15 years out from when they are ultimately going to transition out of their business, translate it's internal value to spendable cash and then move onto whatever's next in their life? What suggestions do you have for them as far as steps they should consider taking, thought processes and who they should consult with to increase the likelihood they'll have an optimal outcome?

Bryan: These are people that are charitable or not charitable?

Adam: Why don't we talk about both? Let's start with someone who's generally charitably inclined at least a little bit and then we can move on from there.

Bryan: First, I know a lot of business owners that don't even have a trust and don't think about their estate at all. If you're in that growth stage where you don't have a lot of assets and you're growing the business, there are things that you can do that are easy to at least cover a lot of the bases. Even going to Christiantrust.com is better than nothing. The second thing is I'd say is never make the oldest kid the executor unless you want your kids to claw each other to hell after your death. Everyone wants to pass along a legacy and all they pass on them when they do that is the kids clawing each other to death. It happens almost without fail. Find someone else to be the executor. Another family member is fine or even a member of your success team. Just don't make your kids the executor... period.

There are a lot of creative things that a person can do with their estate. They don't have to pass it all to their kids. In fact, I just think that's an old, outdated idea is pass it all to kids. Think about what do you actually want to have happen with your assets when you pass away. What is the legacy that you want to pass onto the kids? It should be more than stuff. People in that range of 15 years out from a business transition are starting to think about legacy. The way to think about that is not start with assets. The way to think about that is think about what do you value most? What has meant something to you in your life and how do you want to pass on those values? That's a different conversation than your typical advisor is going to have with you. It requires a different set of ideas than just passing assets.

I also see many business owners start out with a set of advisors and they don't realize that they've outgrown those advisors at some point in time. So they're still using the CPA that is really a great CPA for a $5 million company but not for a $30 million company. They're using a financial advisor who is great at helping families setup 529 accounts for their kids and help couples get out of debt but they're not prepared to oversee the coordination of a legacy plan for a $40M estate. Their relationships cause them to end up having a weaker team simply because of familiarity. I've seen that through my whole career and it's not good. It's okay to have a grown-up conversation with one of your professionals and recognize you need something different.

Finally, the worst story I can think of is a guy I met a few years back that sold his business and left in excess of $25 million paid in taxes. That was just the tax liability. When I showed him what we could have done for him to avoid that entire liability, his immediate response was, "I've got the best advisors money can buy, why didn't anybody tell me about this?".

The right thing to do is ask yourself, "In 15 years what kind of team am I going to need?". That also means not just relying on professionals to do everything for you. It's important to educate yourself in at least the fundamentals of the various issues so you're not just relying on people who may or may not have the best ideas. Round out your success team and demand that they collaborate onto the team so there are checks and balances. Don't just have two people or one person you go to for everything.

You've got to develop enough of a team to where all the bases are covered in the spectrum of financial and life counsel. If you have each of the seats covered that you outlined earlier in the book, rarely is anything going to slip through the cracks, if ever. Too often people don't have enough of the right players around the table when they're far out helping them looking ahead.

Adam: Excellent. Well thanks again Bryan.

Bryan: You're welcome.

Chapter 16: Rick Fenelli, LL.M. Taxation, Attorney at Law, Founder of The Fenelli Law Firm

Rick is the founder of The Fenelli Law firm, a multi-generational law firm focused on the fields of Estate Planning, Tax Planning and Business Planning, Charitable Giving, Estate Administration, and entity formation. He has practiced in Orange County for the past 40 years and has lectured extensively throughout Southern California as the keynote speaker to large corporations, State and County conventions, and life underwriters' conventions, as well as to the general public. He has been a regular on radio stations and has made several television appearances. He is the author of *The Financial Problem Solver*, which is available on Amazon.com and at book retailers nationwide.

Rick attended the University of Oregon where he received his B.A. degree in History. He continued his education at Western State University School of Law where he received his Juris Doctorate degree. He further extended his education by attending classes at the Masters of Business Tax program at USC. He received his LL.M, Masters in Taxation, at Chapman University School of Law in 2007.

Rick and his wife, Margie, have been married for 45 years and are residents of Orange County, California. His daughter, Amy Fenelli Ciftcikara, Attorney at Law, his daughter, Katie A. Fenelli, Attorney at Law, and his daughter, Karianne Welch, Attorney at Law, are all practicing partners in his firm. Rick's two son-in-laws, Oz Ciftcikara and Thomas J. Welch, are Of Counsel to the firm as well. Rick enjoys reading, relaxing in the mountains, taking walks, traveling and spending time with his family, including his nine grandchildren, in his spare time.

The following conversation took place on February 16, 2016 between Rick Fenelli, Attorney at Law, and Adam Broughton, CFP®.

Here's What We Talk About:

- Are certain personality types more likely to be successful in a transition?
- What are some strategies for testing a successor's readiness without giving up control of the company right away?
- What should a founder do different if they are being acquired by a publicly traded company versus a company that's privately held?
- What happens if a founder has multiple children working in the business when he or she is ready to retire?
- What role does insurance play in the succession planning process?
- It planning for taxes the most important part of the transition plan?
- Can a cessation strategy really be a financially beneficial exit plan?
- Plus a whole lot more so read on!

Adam: Hi Rick. What we're discussing today are the transitions business owners go through as they move through their peak earning years and begin thinking about succession. I know you have helped many business owners through this process so I'm hoping you can share some insight into how founders can increase their chances of completing a successful transition.

Rick: Okay, so getting right down to the crux of the issue is this: you don't start looking at a retirement about three months before you want to retire.

Adam: (Laughs) Yeah that usually doesn't work out.

Rick: Too many business owners just don't think far enough in advance. The thing is, you basically have two types of business owners. You have those that are so hands on that they want to control everything and then you have those that have actually gone ahead and set up a team.

The most difficult one to deal with is the owner who is hands on and controlling. The reason being is they have a different outlook and perception about the business. The owner who has a team realizes that he's not the only one who gets credit for making the business what it is today. It took a team to get there. An attitude shift has to take place with the business owner who is 100% hands on. It becomes easier to discuss how the transition can be done when that attitude shift has taken place.

With that in mind, let's examine the first of your three categories – the sale involving an outside buyer. There's good and bad news. The good news is if you're dealing with a buyer that the owner knows personally and who they are confident will be reasonable and act fairly, then it is generally easier to get a deal done. I will come back to this one later.

You also have the other type of outside buyer. There are two subcategories to address here. First, you have a buyer who's basically a publicly traded company. It could be included in the S&P 500, the Dow or it could be on the NASDAQ. The point is they're a publicly traded company. Second, you can have an outside buyer who is not a publicly traded company. They are privately held either by a group of investors or by a family.

When you deal with the publicly traded companies, it's a headache. It's a headache because they have to do an incredible amount of due diligence. They come in and they demand so many different things - one of them being audited financials. That's an expensive proposition. We had to go through this with one of our clients when they were trying to sell the company. The buying company happened to be a publicly traded company. They had all the money in the world to complete the purchase but the problem was they wanted audited financials from the seller. They also wanted to know who all the contracts were with, what the contracts were about and both the seller and the buyer had to sign multiple NDAs (non-disclosure agreements). Our experience has been when you sign the NDA, they often aren't worth the paper they're written on[8].

Adam: No, especially not in California.

Rick: Oh yeah. What happens is you've suddenly "opened up the kimono" and given this outside party all your information. That's a scary proposition to begin with but then, in the case of our client in the story, the buyer proceeded to insult the seller. As his advisors, we knew the business was really worth about $30 million and we had the valuation to back it up. Once the buyer had the information, they said, "Well, we'll pay you $25 million with $5 million held back for earn outs[9] to make sure "other things don't come up.". The specifics of the "other things" that were of concern to the buying company were very nebulous.

Well, this put the seller in a tough spot. The publicly traded company now knew exactly whom the customers were, how the business was run and how to run a business exactly like theirs. They were

---

[8] Each state and jurisdiction views the validity of non-compete and non-disclosure agreements differently depending on the circumstances of the agreement, the relationship between the parties and the scope of the document. Always use extreme caution before divulging confidential or proprietary information to outsiders. Always have a qualified attorney draft and review any legal document prior to use in your business.

[9] An earn out is a common provision in a purchase agreement in which a portion of the sales price is paid over a set future period contingent upon the seller providing ongoing services or helping the buyer achieve certain goals following the transfer of ownership.

competitors. The selling owner, who was more of a hands-on owner, became insulted. I didn't blame him. The deal went nowhere but the seller was left with a problem because he had given so much ammunition to a potential competitor. It could have a major impact on the value of the business whether he kept it or found another buyer.

What we discovered with selling to publicly traded companies is this: I give you the business – it's a going business, you've done your due diligence and had the opportunity to look under every rock. If you then decide to buy the business and subsequently run it into the ground, why should I take on risk for that?

Adam: Right. The reality is: I've done my work to this point. Now it's on you.

Rick: Yes. Here it is. You take this business in "as-is" condition. We've shown you everything you've asked for, so what's the problem? My client was insulted because the buyer came back with an offer well below market value and with multiple contingencies implying there was something wrong with the business.

Adam: So what happened next? Did it fall apart or did they bring the deal together?

Rick: Well, in this case, the brokers got together because they realized now they had to work both sides of the fence. The one broker said to the seller, "You've got to come down on your price because this is the only way of getting the deal done in the terms are reasonable.". Then, the buyer's broker went to the buyer and said, "We've got to come up a little bit because this deal's not going to go through. You need to lighten up on the terms of the earn out.".

Liken it to trying to sell your house. What do the brokers do? Their main job is to negotiate a lower price and a higher price – the lower price from the seller, a higher price from the buyer.

When you have a traded company for a buyer, it becomes very difficult to complete the negotiation because they have their own oversight people. They're answering to Wall Street, they're answering to their bankers, etc. It's very, very difficult on that side to get a deal done.

Look at all the examples in the media of how long it takes traded companies to buy each other. The problem with a publicly traded company (which is usually a large company) trying to buy a smaller privately held company is it's only a matter of time until the cat is out of the bag. It's one thing for Time Warner to announce they are trying to buy America Online. It is unlikely that the merger is going to destabilize everyone in the company. The employees of the selling company either are going to just have a new name on their paycheck or they'll be laid off. There are only two options.

There is greater potential for every person in that smaller organization to be affected when a larger company purchases it. The rank and file begin saying, "Well, if we're going to merge, do we have redundancies? Do we have duplicity in accounting? Do we have duplicity in engineering? Do we have duplicity in sales force?". Suddenly, they're worried about their jobs.

Adam: Right. It's going to affect their productivity.

Rick: Well, productivity to a point. Basically, it affects the morale of the business. Now everybody's saying I better get my resume out there. When you consider the things that can happen when a publicly traded company purchases a privately held company, it isn't an attractive way to complete a transition.

Knowing what we know today, we would simply tell the buyer, "Look, here's the price and the company is available in 'as-is' condition. Here's our information. If you come back to us with less than the price it's worth, then don't even talk to us.". So I find that exit strategy very difficult.

Now, it's different on a private buyer because they're not beholden to Wall Street. They're not beholden to the banks. They simply have to make a business decision. That business decision works better when you have a private buyer because it's easier for the two owners to talk and negotiate. There's less red tape involved.

As a side note, when you bring the business brokers in, all the brokers want to do is make a deal. The seller needs to be aware the broker's incentive is not to put together a deal that is in everyone's best interests. That's what the seller wants. The broker's incentive is to put together *A* deal... period. That's the only way they get paid.

Adam: Well, the only reason to hire one is because you want to make sure a deal gets done. That's what they exist for.

Rick: Whether it's for the seller's benefit or the buyer's benefit, the brokers want to make a deal. They want to make a deal because that's how they're going to get their "cha-ching cha-ching". What we have to do as advisors is be aware of the incentives in place when the brokers come in. They are going to tout themselves when you first meet saying, "Yes we can do this. We can do all of that.". That should be a red flag. The brokers are going to bring the buyer and seller together after making all these promises. Everyone is on his or her best behavior and the seller has been assured it's all going to work out perfectly. That's typically your high point in the deal. Sometimes it feels like the first date.

The first signs of trouble typically show up when the first real offer comes in from the buyer. That's when the real work begins and the buyer and seller have to find out if they're compatible. Depending on how big the gap is in that first offer, they may or may not be able to continue beyond round one. It's just like your first date with your wife. She's going to be decked out in a new outfit, her hair will be done, she'll look beautiful and she'll smell like a flower. If you show up and you haven't combed your hair, you're sweaty from a workout and you are completely rude, you probably won't get a second date with her. You're not compatible even at a foundational level.

Now, there have been cases (like in the real estate world) where you have over bidders. That can cause another set of issues. I'm aware of a case where there was a unique buyer who had a singular purpose for buying a business. It just fit perfectly into this buyer's cog. I was in a meeting several years ago discussing several estate tax matters. There was this one federal estate tax issue that came up when a business owner had passed away. The business was appraised for about $38 million with several offers between $35 million to $40 million for the business. I understood the estate tax return reported a figure of $38 million. Upon the estate sale, an over-bidder bid $70 million for the business and the sale took place.

That is when things started to go sideways for the estate seller. Uncle Sam (the IRS) came back and said, "Wait a minute, this company was not worth between $35 million and $40 million as you said. It was really worth $70 million.". At the end of the day, the client won because they were able to show that it was a business that just happened to fit this particular buyer's business perfectly and they had to have it at any price. The buyer was making sure the seller had no choice but to accept their offer.

They were able to show the $70 million did not represent the common bids that came in. The rest of the bids (about 8 different bids for the company came in) were around the $35 million-$40 million range and then comes this one company willing to pay $70 million. It was a tremendous overbid but they had immediate use and it was going to make their day to be able to integrate this business into their supply chain. That's an unusual situation. But overbids to come out and, while every business owner dreams of getting an offer for twice the appraised value, they need to be aware that even over bids can create issues.

Adam: The more stories I hear the more it drives the point home for me just how critical it is to have a team surrounding you as a buyer or seller who can help you navigate these transitions. You just never know what issues are going to come up in even the simplest deal. What would you say to someone who feels they can handle their transition on their own?

Rick: Absolutely. You have to first understand the basic desire and best-case scenario on both sides of the equation. Every buyer is going to try not to pay anything for the business and every seller wants all his or her cash up front. If I'm selling my house, I don't want to take terms. I want cash. If you're a buyer, you want to put nothing down upfront. You want to put the risk back on the seller. Ideally, you want to stretch out the terms so if the seller has some secrets that pop up later they can then say, "I'm not going to pay you the full amount because this came up and that came up. None of that was disclosed up front.".

The best-case scenarios for either side are often diametrically opposed. You need to have a skilled team in place to navigate the pitfalls and bring the sides closer and closer together until they can each walk away feeling like they got a good deal.

To bring the question full circle, in terms of the outside buyer, there are basically two types. You have the publicly traded companies and you have the private companies. We find that dealing with the private companies is a lot better. Publicly traded companies are a pain in the rear and decrease the odds of success. It doesn't mean it can't be done but sellers need to be aware of what they are getting into up front.

Adam: Great. What about the second type of transition with an internal buyer?

Rick: Well, you pointed out succession planning involves some sort of an internal buy and sell. The best-case scenario is when the founder has done the work already to put a team in place that is equipped to run it in his or her absence. It's much easier to turn it over to a team than even a single person. A lot of ESOPs are built that way and that is one strategy where the seller has tremendous income tax benefits that they can derive if the plan is executed properly. However, if you have a founder who is just at the top of the heap in the company and there's no team in place, they may have a desire to sell it internally but that just doesn't work usually. That poor owner is the bottle washer, he's the chef, he's the maître d' and he's the only person who knows how everything works. Who is there to sell to and what is he or she going to sell them?

So with that in mind, the first question I would ask the business owner is, "Do you have a team in place?".

If so, great! That means you can start making plans to transition more and more responsibility to the team. If not, the emphasis first needs to be on building a team before he or she can start transitioning anything. Not having a team typically means there is considerable prep work to be done before there's any chance of getting financial value out of the business besides ongoing cash flow.

Adam: Sure. That's a longer-term proposition in either case but especially if the seller doesn't have a team in place already.

Rick: Right. That's where I say they need to look ahead five years, like you were saying earlier, and begin building a team that can become the succession plan. However, just like in the outside buyer situation, there are two different kinds of internal buyers as well. There are family and non-family successors.

With family successors, it can create an added layer of headaches. The founder has to determine whether Junior is really going to commit. In cases where there are multiple kids in the business, the founder(s) have to determine which of their kids have both the attitude and the aptitude to continue running the business as an owner. You can have one child who is a total go-getter and is able to take over and run the place. Then you've got two others who are just there to collect their paycheck and otherwise are just bumps on a log. That takes some real emotional honesty on the part of the parents to be able to identify that and address the issues. So few founders have that ability which is why I typically recommend, as you do earlier in the book as well, working with a family coach to bring out those dynamics and ask the right questions that will bring the answers to the surface

Adam: What are some options available to the founders in instances where they have multiple kids in the business and one is a clear successor and the others just aren't there yet (or may never get there)?

Rick: In that case, what I often do is implement a voting/non-voting stock configuration for the underlying entity. If the seller has a C-corporation, we can differentiate the stock as either voting/non-voting or voting stock and preferred stock. If you have a subchapter S-corporation, it will just be voting and non-voting. In limited partnerships and LLC's, it would be a voting interest and a non-voting interest. What we do is reconfigure the existing stock. We're actually doing this right now on several client companies. We reconfigured the stock into a voting/non-voting configuration to address the difference in style and ability between multiple successors.

We first make sure the voting shares go to the person who is actually capable of running the business. Then, we give some additional non-voting stock to that person so they share in distributions and have the remaining non-voting going to the other two less capable/motivated successors so that they can't disrupt the decision making process in the company. In a pass-through entity[10], you'll be able to achieve the same type of revenue streams for everybody but there's a voting and a non-voting stock to make sure the company can continue to run and avoid infighting.

Adam: That's an interesting setup. I'm curious to hear how you address the equalization question because control is one thing but ultimately cash is king. If it's me and my two siblings who don't do anything, I'm happy that they don't have control

---

[10] Pass-through entities are those for which the net income of the organization is not taxed at the entity level and, instead, "passes through" to the individual tax returns of its shareholders or members via K-1.

but I'm not happy that they're profiting off all my hard work. How do you address that?

Rick: Well, you have to go back to the reason why the voting/non-voting was staged. It isn't the child who is driving the setup of the shares. We are setting up that way because that is what the parents want to do.

The parents are most likely going to say, "Listen, we have two choices. We can make you all equal owners and you can fight it out or we can set it up this way and each of you still basically gets what you want.". Nine times out of ten, the more competent successor will respond, "Wait a minute, I don't mind that. We can be even owners. I understand that they're working here. But I've got the voting shares. I have control.".

Here is something key to this solution. When I use the voting/non-voting setup in a succession plan, I also couple it with a very robust buy-sell agreement. That way the plan forces a sale of the non-voting interest to benefit the one who is running the company if the non-voting members don't participate or simply leave the company.

Adam: In that application of a buy-sell agreement, it's not necessarily funded the same way a traditional buy-sell would be with life insurance. So is it executed via a note over a period of years or how do you recommend funding it?

Rick: Well, how you fund it is through a variety of things. Think of an escrow account where the non-voting shares are placed. As long as the payment schedule is made, then the earnings from the non-voting go back to the voting owner. But if the child who holds the voting shares misses a payment (for instance he can't make the payments on it because the company's struggling and he doesn't have the money to do it with) then the non-voting can still stay with the other kids. That's one approach.

The other approach is a clean severing of the ties. The non-voting goes over to the one child and the other two get a note payable from the corporation. The problem with a note payable from the corporation is it's dischargeable in bankruptcy. Then, you have to look at different ways to approach how the non-voting can be done. The other way is for the voting guy to get a loan from the bank to fund the payment out and then he has to work the company to pay back the loan. The other way it's done is that the voting member refinances properties that he has, takes the money out, and then pays off these other people.

The note is probably going to be a combination of cash and financing. The notes we see most often are unsecured [11] in that situation. They're unsecured

---

[11] An unsecured note refers to a loan that is not legally attached to any specific assets of the borrower. The lender is unable to automatically repossess any specific assets of the borrower in the event he or she defaults on the loan. Instead, they would become a general creditor of the borrower and have to sue for repayment or get paid under the terms of a bankruptcy agreement.

because it creates problems for obtaining traditional business financing in the future when you have a secured note against a company. When you go to get a loan in the future, the banker would see there is a lien against the company and typically decline the loan. Secured notes can hobble your successors by preventing access to operating or expansion capital. That's not usually in the successor's best interest or the founder's best interest. What is in everybody's best interest is removing the barriers to growth. So those are some of the ways the buy-sell funding is done.

Now, if the successor is going to have an obligation to pay off a debt, I also suggest looking into insurance for the loan. There are certain insurance policies available to continue the payments to the seller in the event the buyer is unable to perform their job for a period of time due to disability or provide a lump sum in the event the buyer dies. The insurance company can continue to make the payments that are due by the Corporation or pay off the note completely. There are types of insurance policies out there that actually do all of that. I almost always recommend purchasing some type of insurance on the life of both the seller and the buyer as part of the deal. I do that to provide protection for the sellers.

Adam: So that's one strategy for the family succession scenario. What about a non-family succession scenario?

Rick: On the nonfamily succession, it's typical to look first at an ESOP (Employee Stock Ownership Plan) to take care of that. Otherwise, if the success team determines an ESOP isn't a good fit, then what you do is work out the actual payment schedule with the non-family employee. There are a number of ways you can do that as well. I've seen those done with an unsecured note (which we talked about earlier) as well as with a secured note. In the case of the secured note, it's more like purchasing a house. The buyer gets title to the house right away but the lender can take it back if the buyer stops making payments.

I've also seen it done like buying a car and the actual title remains with the seller until the last payment is made. That's when the pink slip (i.e. the ownership) is delivered to the buyer. I suppose that's a good way to differentiate those options: you either buy it as a car or you buy it as a house. It's also possible to transfer some ownership up front to the buyer and the rest at a later time using more exotic planning mechanisms such as restricted stock plans or stock options. Those tend to be more useful for larger companies though and the founders have to be careful to make sure they are incentivizing the right things. It's often more complicated than many founders or successors want the process to be but its still an option.

Adam: That's a good way to think of it.

Rick: Yeah. So the successor can buy it as a car or buy it as a house. If it's setup like buying a house then the seller has a fixed note paying them principal and interest for a period of time. They can be a secured creditor or unsecured creditor in that arrangement. Being an unsecured creditor puts significantly more risk on the seller. If the company is being bought like a car, the seller doesn't give up legal ownership until all payments are made. I have also had the plan set up to where the shares are held in an independent third-party escrow account until the final payment is made.

Let me give you an example. There was a case that came to our office in which two dentists had been in practice together. One of the dentists died unexpectedly. Thankfully, each partner owned a life insurance policy on the other. That million-dollar life insurance policy paid the death benefit immediately to the surviving dentist. The widow then came to the surviving dentist and said, "Here's the stock of the company. I'll take the million dollars.". The surviving dentist refused and never paid the million dollars to the widow. Now, what was wrong there? The problem was the dentists had the insurance but they didn't have a buy-sell document to compel the purchase of the remaining shares from the deceased shareholder's beneficiaries. They had the funding but there wasn't any legal document stating what had to be done with the money. The money should have come to the widow upon the transfer of her deceased husband's interest to the surviving partner. That should have been a key part of the buy-sell agreement.

But you see how little things like that can change the whole outcome? That was a good lesson to learn about how to set up the life insurance beneficiaries within a cross-purchase arrangement. That comes more into play when you have an actual death. The terms of the transfer should be automatic. It's different than a situation involving a transfer of ownership between parties when everyone is still alive. The parties have to make decisions about whether the terms of the note are going to be secured, unsecured, all cash or using terms. You have to figure out which setup is going to work best based on the specific circumstances of the buyer and the seller involved. There's not a one-size-fits-all purchase arrangement and that's again where a top-notch success team becomes so valuable.

Anyway, just to recap, selling to publicly traded companies is usually a pain in the rear. On the internal buyer, you either sell to the team or to family. For the team, you either set up an ESOP or you set financing terms with your internal successor. There is a lot more flexibility and creativity available on a family purchase but also more relational risk.

Adam: Is there anything a founder should be mindful of regarding the tax consequences of those different arrangements?

Rick: Sure. A lot of sellers will go ahead and take terms because they want to pay tax on the capital assets at the time. They choose to do an IRC 454 installment sale where the purchase is done over a period of time. Now, when they take terms over a period of time, one of the best practices that our office does is insist that the seller always purchase a life insurance policy covering the buyer. That way the seller gets their cash in the event the buyer passes away unexpectedly.

What I find is the best arrangements allow us to build hedging into the agreement to protect everyone involved. The first hedging opportunity, as I just said, is if the buyer dies.

I have seen it happen multiple times where the buyer dies a few months or years into the buyout. I always recommend having life insurance on the buyer. That goes for his or her family as well. They need to place sufficient life insurance on the buyer to both pay off the note and provide for his or her family thereafter.

There are different types of insurance policies that will allow you to make the premium payments at a lower level and still be paid out in full. That's where I think the insurance industry has really got it right. They have developed flexible policies that allow buyers to manage their costs while still providing sufficient protection.

I find I have to test temperature of the client when I'm helping them build a succession plan. When I mention we're going to get some insurance to try and cover some of these transactions, they often hit the roof.

What they don't realize is the insurance is their best bet. It's always been their best bet. Life insurance is a miracle product that can give you so many different benefits and cover the myriad contingencies that can and do come up.

Adam: I agree. I come from a fee-based planning background where life insurance has traditionally been looked down on. Personally, I've worked with some insurance agents who obviously were far more concerned about their commission than the outcome for the client. However, the more families I work with and the more succession plans I get involved in, the more obvious the need has become to in my mind to do exactly what you said. You have to hedge the transaction and have a backup plan because things can go sideways quickly and your whole meticulously designed plan and go out the window in an instant.

Rick: Correct. So, just to sum up the different types of buyers, it can be bought internally, with those two options; the family component and the nonfamily component. In the family component, you have lots of opportunities to get creative as long as the relationship is there. In the nonfamily component, if the founder has not invested time building a team and still has the idea that he is going to be successful in selling it internally, he's up a creek without a paddle.

In that situation, you often end up going out the third door you talked about. When does it make sense to go to a cessation strategy? We go there when no one's going to be there to buy it internally or externally for any number of reasons. For example, when there's no market for the company. We then have to examine how to best "wind it down".

Now, when you wind down a company (meaning you are going to close it and terminate the entity), the thing founders have to be aware of is the different tax rates that will be applied to the assets in the business. Someone has to identify what your intellectual property assets are, what your ordinary income assets are and what your long-term capital gain assets are.

An accounting professional has to do an analysis because, when you wind down a company, you're typically going to have a tax basis[12] issue. Either the assets are worth more than the basis or they're worth less than the basis. Those are numbers that have to be thought through in terms of a cessation strategy. Interestingly, in California, when you cease a company, the Franchise Tax Board (FTB) comes in and says, "Mr. or Mrs. Owner, we want you to take over all of the tax liabilities that may come through at some point in the future.". Also, owners need to be aware that may not off the hook in terms of liability when they cease a business. Welcome to the real world.

---

[12] Tax basis is an accounting term, which generally describes the total dollar amount the taxpayer spent to acquire an asset. It includes the purchase price itself but determining your basis can require a few adjustments so I'll leave the full explanation to your tax pro!

Adam: That's a surprise to a lot of business owners. They can still be subject to liability years down the road in a lawsuit against their company that no longer exists.

Rick: Well, the business owner needs to have the accountant or the lawyer determine whether it makes sense to officially close the business with the FTB. The FTB will say, "Fine, we'll terminate the entity but we don't know if you have any outstanding tax liabilities. You're still responsible for anything that arises in the future pertaining to this defunct entity.".

Adam: In your opinion, is it better not to terminate the corporation and leave it running just as an inactive entity for a period of years until all of the potential liabilities are known?

Rick: Sometimes it is advisable to keep the company inactive for several years to see what potential liabilities might come up. Here's something it is important for a *BUYER* to consider: If they are buying the stock of a company that will include all the assets, a buyer needs to be especially cautious. By buying all the stock of the company, they are also taking over all the future liabilities of the company whether tax or otherwise. When a buyer purchases only the assets of the company, the buyer should consider doing a bulk sale transfer. There are a variety of reasons for that but certain newspaper publications should also be notified to alert the general public that a sale is taking place. They should notify the public that now is the time to bring a claim if the seller owes any monies to them.

That's why most people don't typically buy the shares of the company. They actually just buy the assets. Traded companies are more inclined to buy the company because they want to keep it as a subsidiary. That is also why publicly traded companies go through the grueling due diligence process I mentioned. It's because they're usually actually buying the company itself rather than just the assets.

Adam: Talk to me about the tax differences when selling the company stock versus the company assets.

Rick: The best thing for a seller is to have a buyer purchase the company stock because the seller gets long-term capital gain treatment. There may be some hidden tax issues such as hidden recapture issues that create ordinary income tax when they could've been capital gain when a buyer only purchases the assets of a company. Further, depending on the type of company you have (C Corporation, subchapter S-Corporation, partnership or LLC), different taxes may be imposed to the company by reason of the sale of the assets. Tax issues come with the territory in business transitions and you need a good accounting team to help navigate those issues.

For the cessation of a business that a). is a pass-through entity and b). has a lot of assets, it may make sense just to terminate the corporation and pass the tax treatment to the founder. Those are all things that can be done. We've had several businesses that had a chance to sell but the seller was adamant about selling on a tax-favorable basis. They went through a series of complex tax planning gyrations before the sale went through in an attempt to make it as tax free as possible. The end result was a tax-free sale but it majorly affected the value of the company to the negative. We did the analysis afterward and determined they would have made the same amount of money they wound up getting in the sale within three years if they had just kept the business. They could have then either shut it down after three years or used that time to develop an internal team for a succession strategy.

That speaks to the reality that it doesn't always make sense to sell net of tax. In some instances, the advice would be to focus on developing a great team so you can take time off and become a semi-retired absentee owner. At some point, you can go into a voting/non-voting setup like I discussed earlier and gradually start giving the team (the nonfamily member team) some of the non-voting stock so they get direct benefits of their work.

The counter-balance to the team succession strategy is there must be limits on what the absentee owner can do. You don't want the founder (who owns the voting stock) to just show up out of nowhere and vote himself a million-dollar bonus one day. You need to put limits in place to protect the team. It's a good idea to put thresholds in place to make sure that the team who's putting in the sweat equity eventually receives equity that is valuable. Usually, I set it up so the sweat equity earners have the right to buy the voting stock after five years and then the absentee owner can officially be out of the business. That makes a lot of sense and I've seen a lot of small businesses do that.

Adam: I've seen that especially come into play especially with startup companies where the entrepreneur has what I call "founder syndrome". There's a founder who is a serial entrepreneur and is used to pulling money out of the company whenever he wants it and however much he wants. Then he starts trying to get venture capital money involved and also trying to build an internal team. One day he gets the urge to buy a new house/car/business/whatever and decides to write himself a check for half a million bucks. The team who has been working 80 hours/week is sitting there going, "Hey, you can't just come in here because you want to buy the newest toy and pull money out of the company. That doesn't work. We're the ones who generated that revenue while you've been off 'vision casting'.". When that kind of conflict starts occurring, it's the beginning of the end unless major changes happen.

The reality is the founder has to be willing give up some of that control if he or she wants to make this a sustainable business. That's a mature mindset focused on laying the ground for a succession strategy. So that's a situation where that can be useful to set those caps and thresholds in place like you were saying. But it can be a difficult sell, especially with a serial entrepreneur who is used to calling the shots and taking what they need.

Rick: That's where they can get into a preferred stock relationship where the preferred stock always gives them a dividend or gives them pass through income, which I think makes some sense. Another good way I've seen it done is going to an "X-plus" arrangement when you're dealing with these owners who are trying to get their businesses ready to go to the next generation or transition to a team. For example, I was involved with transition plan where the owner told his team, "Look, you send me X amount of dollars per month. Anything over that, you keep.". It was a very simple proposition. He wanted $30,000 in monthly profits. There was $60,000 a month in profits on average so the other $30,000 went to the team. Very interesting, very simple and it worked! As long as they ran the business and the founder got his $30,000 a month, the team got the rest. It was darn near perfect. What I'm saying is there's always ways to do the deal. It just takes an advisor who understands the goals and the constraints of the company.

Adam: What are some of the key questions you feel an owner needs to have answers to before they start down this path? What do they need to have total clarity on?

Rick: Well, the first question to be determined is this: Does the founder need the money from the business to fund his or her lifestyle or have they done such a good job of planning they could still exist if the company went down the drain? That's the first question you've got to have clarity on because that gives the success team direction as to how to setup the plan. Let's take the one end of the spectrum where the business is the founder's sole income and its cash value is the primary income source for their future lifestyle. In that case, the team is going to have to design the plan in a way that allows the owner to have the confidence that he or she is going to be able to have consistent money coming in because that's all he or she has to live on. That limits the options as to how the transition can be designed and what risks they can take.

The next question to ask is, "How much decision-making authority are you willing to share before you're paid in full?". As I've mentioned before, I always suggest building an internal team that is empowered to make decisions and run the business without the founder's presence. However, that's often in direct contrast to what the business owner is thinking. As soon as I mention building a team to a hands-on owner, the response I get is, "I don't want to give up control". The desire to maintain full control is another limiting factor in how the transition plan can be designed. If full control is a non-negotiable, that's where the voting/non-voting conversation comes in again.

The success team has to get clarity on those two concepts first to know where to take the planning. Then they can help the business owner build more of his or her personal assets, their personal revenue streams, identify which of the three doors could be a good fit, etc. That information allows the success team to mitigate some of the risk of a complete business failure turning into a lifestyle disaster.

A third type of business owner is someone who's built up his or her financial fortress outside the business (because they've been working with someone like you, Adam) but is also committed to getting full market value for the business. That opens up a different set of strategies on the planning landscape. In that case, what I typically look at is the income component the founder IS looking for even though they aren't solely relying on the cash value of the business.

That scenario means I can begin to explore more creative, flexible strategies. It also makes life a little easier for the internal management team who will be running the business or the outside person coming in. It means they can more easily pay the exiting owner and still run the business (in case it's not an all-cash deal) because they don't have such heavy cash flow drag. It's always easiest when the founder has outside assets or streams of revenue to support their lifestyle.

Adam: Of course. Most founders are going to want all cash up front so they can walk away and not have to rely on someone else for their income. The problem is very few buyers are willing to offer all cash. I'm not sure what the statistics are but my guess would be it's less than 10% of deals are all cash for privately held businesses.

Rick: Correct. They're your best deal for the seller but few buyers want to pay all cash.

Adam: Right. There's too much liability involved for the buyer.

Rick: It's not necessarily about the liability. Especially when the buyer really understands what's going on inside the business he or she is buying. It's more often about the potential for business attrition and the buyer doesn't want to have paid full price for a business that's only worth 80% or 60% of that amount six months later.

For example, when we buy out a law practice, we will only pay a percentage of what we earn back to the seller because we expect some level of attrition (meaning some clients may leave). We had to do that when we purchased the practice of a lawyer who died unexpectedly. For example, we could agree to pay out

30% of the gross billings that we receive from the new client base for the first three years. That's what goes to the seller or the surviving spouse. That's a pretty standard arrangement. It's still a good deal because the seller is getting her money out but all the headaches are on us. Sometimes it's 20% for 4 years but some type of arrangement like that is common in professional practices.

The bottom line it has to be a win-win for both sides. This idea of a founder who is going to squeeze every penny out of the buyer needs to go away. Whenever people put together a win-win situation, they can buffer the storms. But to me, it comes down to that one basic question. Do you need this to live on, to pay your bills? Or do you have other assets outside that can take the place of it?

The last piece that has to be considered by the success team is the intangible part, which is the emotional stuff. I understand taking pride in your business. But there are some people out there who have completely wrapped up their identity in the business. They act like they're the only ones responsible for the success of the business and no one can do it better than them. Well, they're generally wrong. That type of person is almost impossible to help.

Adam: I call that the Tigger syndrome. Their mantra is, "I'm the only one.".

Rick: [Laughs] I call it the Picasso syndrome. Picasso could make a painting and sell it for $4 million. If you don't want to pay $4 million for it, then find somebody else. How many Picassos are really out there?

Adam: Only so many.

Rick: Exactly. Most founders aren't a proverbial Picasso and there's almost always another option out there for a buyer. The seller can't go around acting like they've got a corner on the market or the buyer should be grateful to them for something. There's always another option out there that's usually just as good. If there isn't yet, aggravating a potential buyer is a good way to ensure there will soon be a new competitor entering the market.

Good business doesn't just mean you work hard. You definitely need to work hard and put your time in. You also must develop your skills in leadership. You need to make sure you work daily with your rank and file employees and talk to your direct reports. You have daily huddling and you make sure everybody is following the core values that you have developed. That's the sort of team environment you want to have in place when you leave.

The best founders also know how to address issues in the business without destroying their team. I call it care-frontational leadership, Adam. Not confrontational. Care-frontational. A care-frontational leader knows he or she can't be judgmental in order to make the business work. Their desire is to leave it in a position so it can go ahead and grow 100 times more than what they did rather than have their tenure at the helm be the high water mark as a tribute to their own greatness. The greatest joy for any seller should be to see their company grow to be worth 100 times more than what they sold it for. It means everybody won.

Adam: That seems to be the mark of someone who's a giver instead of a taker as you and I have talked about in past discussions. A giver is going to find joy in being able to say, "I'm excited that someone else has been able to build on what I started. They were more successful than I ever was with it and that's fantastic!".

A taker is going to be on the other side saying, "See, I should've gotten more for it than he paid me. I was cheated because he knew exactly what he was going to do with it and he gave me a low-ball offer knowing what it would be worth in five years. I should have held out for more.". Then the lawsuits start. Everybody loses.

Rick: That's right. The taker is always going to think they got taken advantage of no matter what. The bottom line is they really aren't being taken advantage of. It's just that someone else brought a different skillset, which allowed the business to grow to another level. Other people have different avenues, different connections, different ways of looking at it and different response to the market conditions that are available.

Adam: What other questions do you feel founders need to be aware of when considering a transition out of their business?

Rick: The other thing I tell business owners is never to do a deal solely for tax reasons. Do it for the economic reasons. Many people attempt to set up convoluted transactions just to save taxes and wind up blowing up the deal and their business. They end up putting proverbial handcuffs on the next generation in many cases. The tax side of the deal shouldn't be driving the strategy. Think of your deal like water flowing down hill. Take the path of least resistance if possible. If a seller can get all cash, they should take their cash, pay capital gains rates and move on. I've had too many people try to do tax maneuvers that ultimately broke up the deal. It's important to have the tax professional and charitable giving expert involved but they shouldn't be in the lead role.

As an example, I had a client several years ago that owned several rental properties that he wanted to sell. He came to me and said, "Listen, I'm going to get about $1.4 million for these properties. I'm going to pay $200,000 in taxes and I'll end up with $1.2M.". I told him to take the deal right away. He looked at me and said, "I don't want to pay the $200,000.".

Here's what he did instead: He did a 1031 exchange[13] into a TIC, (a tenant in common relationship) on the advice of some financial advisor. The particular TIC he invested his money in happened to be a large, well-known provider that recently ended up going bankrupt. He lost 100% because he wanted to save 30%. The tax result was the highest priority. What I feel about tax planning for major business deals is this: If you made a profit and you can pay capital gain tax on it, take that deal all day long and put the money in the bank. Don't complicate it with esoteric tax planning strategies because you're likely to wind up spending more in court costs, legal fees and representation before the IRS than you would have spent in tax.

Too many people try to construct absurd tax structures. Sometimes you just make a decision to "pay the freight". You made money and you pay the tax on it and call it a day. Now, a part of that money coming to you is going to be return on investment, return of principal. And the other part will be gain.

So you know what? Sometimes you just pay the tax. The economic bottom line takes priority over the tax bottom line when you're selling a business or when you're buying a business.

---

[13] 1031 exchange refers to a section of the US Tax Code governing tax-free exchanges of like kind property. This is another one to talk to your tax professional about for a full explanation if you're unfamiliar with the strategy.

Adam: It strikes me that having clarity on what the overall most important goals are at the outset is absolutely critical. It gives you an anchor point to look back at to determine how far off the mark your plan is or how close it is. It is so easy to get lost in the weeds on little details. Tax issues are especially distracting and founders can end up missing out on the bigger picture because they're so focused on this one small issue.

Rick: That's one of the greatest benefits of having the attorney and the CPA involved in the planning. The attorney and CPA have to go at it and arm wrestle and figure out how to do things.

Adam: Of the three options mentioned – Sale, Succession or Cessation – which would you say is the easiest and which is the most difficult to successfully pull off?

Rick: I've been involved in all three of these - the selling to an outside buyer, selling to the people inside, and also liquidation. The easiest one, in my opinion, is dealing with the family because the parents usually want to give the kids a break and the kids typically aren't going to take advantage of the parents. And, of course, we always have the little joke where the parents say to the kids, "Well, if you foul this thing up, all the other assets in their trusts are going to go to someone other than you.". It's said partially in jest but the serious element is the parents can hold something over the kids to make sure everyone plays nice.

Adam: [Laughs] Yeah, it makes for awkward dinner conversation at Thanksgiving if you screw your family over too badly.

Rick: That's right. I feel when you're selling to an outside person, that's the most difficult. I think the liquidation is really the last resort and I think selling to the inside family member or team member is the best option for most companies if they have the time and discipline to do it right. That's been our experience with our clients.

Adam: What are your thoughts on when and how to go about obtaining a valuation for a closely held business?

Rick: The earlier the better, frankly. The first thing is you have to get the business appraised to get a basis for what an outside person will be looking at. It's not uncommon for the founder/owner to feel the business is worth $100 million and it's only worth $2 million. It happens all the time. The owners have so much "blue sky" [14] written into the valuation and they don't realize a buyer isn't going to see that number the way they do. For example, in major law firms, a partner's partnership interest really isn't worth that much. A

---

[14] Blue sky is a term used to describe the intangible portions of a business' value. It can include things like the business' reputation, the length and strength of its customer or client relationships or the public's perception of the brand. Blue sky is typically given a financial value in a formal valuation but it can be highly subjective.

CPA firm is a little different because you have repeat business so you can quantify it a little bit easier based on the revenues that are done over a period of time. A CPA should get some payout based on those factors but if a lawyer or other professional is relying upon their partnership interest to be their big payday, forget about it. It just doesn't work that way. Those types of businesses are often 99% blue sky because so much of the revenue is generated as a result of the relationship with that specific person. There's no brand value.

Adam: It all comes down to the client relationship in a service-based business like that. That's really where the value is but that relationship is especially difficult to actually put a value on.

Rick: Sure because a client can go away tomorrow.

Adam: Right, it's 100% up to the client in that case whom they want to continue working with. All this nonsense about non-competes and making claims as to who supposedly owns which clients in most professional service businesses is pointless. If the founder hasn't done the work of building a business that clients will come back to regardless of which advisor, doctor, dentist, lawyer, tax preparer or real estate agent sits down with them, the valuation for that business isn't worth the paper it's printed on. Relationships have value to the people who are actually involved in them. If one person goes away, the relationship is worthless.

Rick: The business valuation issue comes down to two basic questions:

#1 - How do you value your business as a whole?

#2 - How do you value each component of the business independently?

A buyer is interested in the company for a reason. They're coming because they know that type of business and they think they can either grow its value or they believe it will add value to one of their existing businesses.

Adam: There's so much self-awareness and humility required on the part of a seller when they're approaching any kind of a transition in their business. As you alluded to, ego issues are waiting around every corner to foul up the whole deal. Founders need to have the self awareness to say, "Yes, I built my business over the last 10, 20, or 30 years, but I know that I need help to successfully complete this transition. I know its time to hand over the reins. I know I don't have all of the best ideas for taking it into the next level.". That requires a great deal of humility on the part of the seller.

Rick: Well, the two conflicting forces in any business transaction are fear and greed. The greed component says, "I deserve a lot more.". The fear component says, "What if X, Y or Z happens? I should keep things as they are instead.". Fear and greed. These emotions come into every deal and the founder has to be able to deal with them appropriately. When Warren Buffet buys a business, he looks at the balance sheet, does his due diligence, makes a decision and that's it. He has gotten to the point where he's taken most of emotion and ego out of the equation.

Every founder is different though in their ability to deal with their emotions and keep them out of a deal. There was Armand Hammer who was the President of Occidental Petroleum. He was going to run that company until the day he died and that's exactly what happened. Sumner Redstone had the same situation with Viacom. The former owner of the Los Angeles Clippers, Donald Sterling, is another good example of what happens when a person isn't in control of his or her emotions. These individuals had major companies to run and they each had the ego to match. They all lost in the end.

Adam: The most important thing I feel founder's need to be able to do is take their ego out of the equation, find the price that they can live with and then move forward.

Rick: That's right. Now, I recall the method of the sale of the Anaheim Angels from Gene Autry to Disney. According to CBS news, in 1996, Mr. Autry sold a minority interest in the Angels to Disney for a down payment with the right to buy the remaining interest when Mr. Autry passed away. He paid tax on the upfront down payment. Then, when he passed away in 1998, CBS news reported that Disney bought the remaining interest. The total price was reported to be $147 million in two phases.

What is important to know for owners of a company, however, is that when Mr. Autry passed away, the remaining interest got a full stepped up tax basis. That meant no income tax on the majority of the proceeds and the transfer to Mrs. Autry was estate tax free. That was an example of the economics and tax planning at the same time working well together.

Adam: However, before the tax planning ever entered into it, Autry had to settle in his own mind what was most important. He had to have it worked out in his heart that any structured deal was going to accomplish what was most important to them. Then their advisors said, "Okay, we can accomplish all of those things *AND* we can put it in a very tax efficient wrapper.". There could have been other ways to make it happen but the focus was on the goals of the Autry family. Everything else was flexible.

Rick: Flexibility is probably the next rule of business transitions. You can get all the appraisals you want but it's going to be a willing buyer, willing seller, each seeing the benefits of the deal and then designing the financing arrangements to incorporate flexibility in case things change. Look at all these big corporations that go bankrupt because their deals were financed with debt. It turned out they took on way too much debt and when business conditions changed even slightly, it took the whole company down. They had no flexibility or additional margin for error.

Adam: I'm sure the future looked bright at the time. All of the assumptions built into a business deal are based on the combination of unique perspectives of the buyer and the seller. Think of them trying to drive a car together. The buyer is always looking forward at the road ahead and basing his or her assumptions about the value of the business on future expectations for growth. The seller is looking in their rearview mirror at everything that they've done in the past and basing their beliefs about the business' value on what went into the business up to this point. They've got to find someplace to meet.

Those two viewpoints are in tension with one another but it's a necessary tension. The multi-billion dollar valuations being put on startups like Uber and Twitter are good examples of what happens when there's only one perspective being considered. It's clear in those cases that only the forward-looking perspective is being considered for the valuation. Discerning buyers will understand that and ask, "Who is looking forward and who is looking backward? Exactly where is that value coming from?".

Rick: Even when the valuation does come back, sellers and buyers still have to sit down and ask, "How can we make this really work?". The practical issues then have to be hashed out once a valuation has been established.

Adam: Talk to me about timing for a transition. When does the founder need to start thinking about transition planning?

Rick: When the business is going good and you are in peak earning years, look to sell. Start looking to sell or transition at that point because that's when buyer is going to see the business as having the most value. There is recent history and evidence to support the valuation. If business is really going well, those are the times when you're most likely to find a buyer willing to pay all cash. The founder can get his or her cash and move on to the next phase of life. It's usually too late when business is slow or when there's been a crisis. The founder (or his or her family) can't expect full value at that point. They have to be willing to deal.

There was a company by the name of Pioneer Takeout Chicken years ago that was a competitor to Kentucky Fried Chicken. I used to deliver chickens to them back in 1972 while going to law school and we delivered to the Pioneer Takeout. The founder had grown to over 200 locations in Southern California. I heard that a major company had an interest in buying out the entire interest and the price was for many millions of dollars. I recall figures that could have approached $50 million. No sale took place.

Adam: Fifty million in 19 – what year was that?

Rick: I think 1981 or 1982.

Adam: Wow. So that's somewhere between $150M to $200M in today's dollars?

Rick: Yeah. It's a big number. The owner of Pioneer Takeout Chicken purchased and built the town of Blue Jay near Lake Arrowhead in California. He built it. Well, his company today is bankrupt. Imagine if he had gotten a tax-free transfer into the stock of that major potential buyer in 1981?

Adam: That would've been a good deal.

Rick: When they have a business that's very successful, owners/founders tend not to know when to sell. They simply keep riding the wave. They go back out and surf again. Pretty soon they're 65 or 70 years old and both they and the company are past their prime. Every founder never thought they were going to sell ever. This is their baby. They were going to raise the business. They were going to nourish it. They were going to provide for it and someday they figured the sweat equity would somehow provide for them as long as they took care of it. Before you know it 30 years goes by like with me. It doesn't happen that way though. They have to translate that sweat equity into spendable, personal wealth at some point and that means making a transition somewhere along the way.

The time to start that transition planning is years before you're ready to actually step out the door. The best time to do it is when things are going well in the business. Now, I'm lucky because I have my three daughters who are all lawyers. I can't tell you how my lawyer friends look at me. They're very envious (in a nice way) because most don't have anybody to pass on their sweat equity to.

Adam: You're definitely fortunate in that regard. You've got a great family and your daughters know what they're doing. You have confidence you're leaving it in good hands because you have been diligent to bring them into the business early and hand over responsibility along the way. That's a huge advantage to you. Well, I really appreciate you being a part of this book, Rick. Your insight has been so helpful.

Rick: You're welcome, Adam.

Chapter 17: Now That You Know, What Should You Do?

Congratulations to you for coming this far! Reading all the way to the end of this book means either a). you have ample time on your hands or b). succession planning is something you are either actively involved in or will soon be involved in. I have a few next steps you need to take as follows:

1. Take the *Free Business Transition Assessment* found in Appendix A at the back of this book The Free Business Transition Assessment is a tool I've developed to help you gauge your readiness to make a transition in your own business. You can complete it in less than two minutes and it is powerful. If you are one of several partners in your company, make copies of the quiz or email each of them a link to the website to complete it on their own. Review your results together ONLY after each partner has completed it on his or her own.

2. Consider scheduling an assessment call with me. I offer a complimentary 30-minute assessment review call to review and discuss the results of the 10-question quiz. Those ten questions are the fastest way to evaluate where you are in your transition planning process, what your likelihood of success is and identify where I can provide the most value to

you and your family. Assessments can be booked online at www.strategysessionwithadam.com.

3. Share this book with someone who needs it. We all know that man or woman who goes 110% all the time in their business. They may be making more money than ever before and seem as though life is great. You may wonder, "Why would they want to think about exiting their business?" Trust me: They need to read this book and they need to start planning. It may also be someone you know who has mentioned they'd like to retire from their business but aren't sure where to start. This book is for them as well. Lastly, perhaps you know someone who has an emergency situation and urgently needs to exit their business. There can still be value in this book for them.

I had a business owner approach me after one of my speaking events and ask when I thought the best time was for him to plan his transition out of the business. My first response was, "No less than a year before you plan to have a heart attack, the economy tanks or your largest customer leaves you for a competitor." He smiled and asked, "Well, how am I supposed to know when that's going to happen?". I told him, "Exactly. You need to start planning today because you won't know exactly when the right time was until it's in the rearview mirror."

The best way to improve your chances of maximizing the value of your business and transforming it into a lifetime of personal wealth for your family is to plan when you have the luxury of planning. That means starting well before you intend to leave, before you're too sick to come to work anymore and before you absolutely need the money for your retirement.

Thank you again for picking up this book. I sincerely wish you the best in your own succession planning efforts and hope I get the opportunity to hear the story of your business someday.

Appendix A – The Pre-Transition Assessment

Question: Could You Exit Your Business Tomorrow And Maintain Your Desired Lifestyle For A Lifetime?

Read Each Statement Below and Respond	Yes/No
1. My company has documented our value-critical processes, products and personnel.	
2. I have established a valuation trend for my business going back at least three years.	
3. I am confident my spouse and/or children would know what to do if I died or was incapacitated tomorrow.	
4. My employees have been cross-trained in the specific aspects of my job and could effectively perform my role if I could not show up for work tomorrow.	
5. We have incentive plans in place to retain value-critical personnel for at least the next five years.	
6. My emergency plan is funded with sufficient life insurance to provide cash for my successors to continue operating the business *AND* provide lifetime income for my family.	
7. All company owners have a written plan for generating retirement income that does not depend entirely on the sale of the business (i.e. is funded with substantial assets outside the business).	
8. My professional advisors understand my long-term legacy and financial goals *AND* collaborate effectively to help me achieve them.	
9. I am confident my personal estate plan is aligned with my wishes regarding who should have control of my company upon my death.	
10. I have identified at least one other company whose values are aligned with ours and whose processes, products and services are complimentary to ours.	

Appendix B – Assessment Grading Scale

Scoring

7 or More "Yes" Answers: You Are Almost There!

You have a high likelihood of being able to maintain your lifestyle in retirement. However, it is important to review your plan regularly and make adjustments as business conditions and life circumstances change.

4 – 6 "Yes" Answers: There Is Still Work To Do.

Industry data indicates a few changes to your current planning could significantly increase your odds of a successful exit from your business and decrease your risk of a complete business failure in the event of the unexpected departure of an owner.

Less Than 4 "Yes" Answers: WARNING!

There are dangerous gaps in your exit & retirement plan. Business owners with less than 4 "yes" responses have a very low chance of exiting their business and maintaining their desired lifestyle without making substantial changes. They are also at significant risk of experiencing a complete business failure following an owner's unexpected departure.